MY HUSBAND,
Jimmie Rodgers

MY HUSBAND, JIMMIE RODGERS

BY CARRIE RODGERS

INTRODUCTION BY NOLAN PORTERFIELD

Country Music Foundation Press

Nashville, Tennessee

Country Music Foundation Press

222 Rep. John Lewis Way South

Nashville, Tennessee 37203

Originally published in 1935 by the San Antonio Southern Literary Institute.

Second Edition published 1953. Third edition published 1975.

Fourth Edition published 1995. Fifth edition published 2023.

First CMF Press edition published in 1975.

Library of Congress Control Number: 2023941447

ISBN 978-0-915608-41-6

To Our Daughter

ANITA

Her Father's Pal and Inspiration,

I Lovingly Dedicate This Book

The voice that reached a million hearts

Is in this whirling disc of black!

Though stilled forever, it returns

To bring beloved memories back

Of one whose mission was to heal

The pain when Fortune's darts were hurled;

The voice that dried a million tears

Returns to soothe a lonely world.

Mary Beth Fagett

INTRODUCTION

1

It is no exaggeration to describe Jimmie Rodgers as "legendary," for even in his own lifetime he had been elevated to something of a folk-hero, and the cultural deification of America's Blue Yodeler has continued over the years, undiminished by time or true revelation.

Jimmie Rodgers's life has been particularly susceptible to romanticizing, marked as it was by his humble origins, sudden success, fame and wealth, his early, tragic death—all the things which appeal to our sense of drama and destiny, the stuff out of which we spin our popular gods and goddesses, our Bixes, our Marilyns, our Scotts and Zeldas, our James Deans, and Hank Williamses. But while the lives of the great and famous are invariably subject to distortion, rarely has the truth suffered more from our natural compulsion to mythologize our heroes than in the case of James Charles Rodgers, The Singing Brakeman, America's Blue Yodeler, pride of Meridian, Mississippi, "father" of country music.

There are many reasons for the fables and fabrications. One was Jimmie himself; in his own genial, harmless way, he originated or let stand endless stories about his life and career, and it mattered little to him if they depicted him as a saint or sinner, so long as they caught the flavor of his own self-image and added to his notoriety. Then, too, his appeal was largely to an audience whose literary tradition was oral rather than written, people who told stories rather than read them. Their respect for what may be called "literature," their deep and abiding involvement with the annals of human experience, was no less great than that of a sophisticated city audience, but it took different forms, with different, often paradoxical consequences. It meant, for one thing, that while they cherish the most extravagant stories and rumors about their idols, they were at the same time uneasy with, if not downright distrustful of, books; of anything which "published" the story or event, made it public, fixed it with the weight of authority or scholarship.

INTRODUCTION

And finally, it was part of Rodgers's peculiar magic that thousands who saw him perform or merely bought his records so immediately identified with him that they became long-lost friends or relatives, and told them what they knew: of their dear old mother who raised Jimmie, of the time Jimmie 'invented" the yodel, of Jimmie singing his way out of jail (over and over), of Jimmie on his deathbed, issuing fond remembrances and deathless last words. He was Will Rogers's son, and Roy Rogers's father—or perhaps it was the other way around. His romantic exploits would have exhausted a robust satyr (and utterly defied a frail "lunger" dying of tuberculosis); his "cousins," boyhood pals, and illegitimate children would have populated a small city.

At the opposite extreme was the "official" version, straight out of Horatio Alger and the Great American Dream: Jimmie Rodgers, the poor but honest country lad, orphaned at a tender age, who struggled determinedly against great odds, became an overnight success, a national idol, but somehow remained pure and undefiled, resisted the temptations of the bright lights and gay ladies, kept himself above the giddy whirl of show business—Jimmie Rodgers, loving husband and father, he of the robe and slippers, fireplace, and faithful bulldog.

The truth, as usual, was somewhere in between, but this double vision of Jimmie Rodgers as rakehell-and-homebody was itself a vital part of the legend, an inevitable result of the curious standard of "honesty" which has historically afflicted the cultural institution known today as "Country Music." It is a standard which honors as fact the wildest myths and most scurrilous gossip about the private lives of its heroes, yet at the same time insists upon a public image that is pure and noble. As Jimmie Rodgers put it, reversing the emphasis, "If they like you when you're nice, they'll forgive you when you're naughty." It was an attitude he understood only too well, and one he often traded upon.

This double standard, however, presents formidable hazards to anyone who would seriously examine or write about country music and its "stars," for among

INTRODUCTION

fans it carries with it a high tolerance for fabrication, omissions, and outright false-hoods so long as they embellish the hero's stature, while on the other hand any overt statement short of absolute idolatry is criticism and the slightest inaccuracy in an innocent detail is cause enough to question the critic's motives, if not, indeed, his patriotism and ancestry. The situation is especially crucial when it comes to Jimmie Rodgers, only begetter of it all, and the object of so many myths and legends be-loved by his friends and fans. They will quarrel heatedly with an obscure newspaper account which misspells the name of a distant Rodgers kin, and in the next breath repeat as though it were scripture another of the old bromides about Jimmie giving his guitar to a crippled newsboy.

The sad fact is that, beyond press agent puffery and the shallow panegyrics of fan magazines, for years very little of Jimmie Rodgers's life-and-time was committed to print, and until the late 1970s there was almost nothing that was both comprehensive and reliable. In this void, Carrie Williamson Rodgers's book, *My Husband, Jimmie Rodgers*, stands as a supremely important, if somewhat curious, document—one that is at once informative and evasive, honest and fanciful, profound and trivial, a subjec-tive personal memoir and an effort toward straight biography. Its author called it "the history of his life and musical career in story form" [1] (and one can hardly refrain from pondering the possible implications of these terms, of what happens when "history" is written in "story form"). To country music scholar Bill Malone, the book is "romanti-cized and sanitized," and other commentators have criticized it for being sentimental, rarely specific, and prone to conflicting accounts of controversial details and events. [2] The terms are accurate, but they do not tell the whole story. *My Husband, Jimmie Rodgers* is the unique expression of a rather unique woman, and its vagaries as well as it virtues derive from the unusual circumstances of the author's life, the very circumstanc-es without which she could not, in either form or content, have written such a book.

INTRODUCTION

2

From early in life, Carrie Cecil Williamson was exposed to many seemingly anomalies. A minister's daughter, she nevertheless grew up in a home that was far more liberal and sophisticated than the time and place would appear to have allowed—"none of your stern, sour fanatics," as she wrote. The seventh of nine children, she occupied no special place among her siblings; she was prettier than most of them but less talented, quiet and reserved to the point of shyness yet fiercely independent. The 1918 Meridian City Directory lists: "Carrie Williamson, slsldy, b[oards] 1609 11 ave [the family residence]." She was barely sixteen and still in school, holding a fulltime clerk's job and paying her own living expenses. It was about this time that she met the lanky young "brakie" with an infectious grin, a line of gab, and precious little else except the vague notion that, someday, he was "going places." [3]

The presence of Jimmie Rodgers in her life immensely complicated things for Carrie Williamson. It was a clear case of the attraction of opposites. He was just about everything that she was not: high-spirited, gregarious, recklessly impulsive, carefree, and absolutely careless with whatever came his way, whether it was his money, his health, or his friends. He soon came to respect at least one thing—his talent—but in those days it may have been simply his peculiar brand of independence, so different from Carrie's, which appealed to her—or perhaps it was nothing more than his cheerful optimism and his jaunty grin. Together they overcame, or simply went around, her family's objections (which were far more intense than she even hints at in the book), only to face far greater and more prolonged obstacles. Mostly it was Jimmie's habitual inability to rub two nickels together; whenever he got them, he spent one and gave the other away. That was when he could find work. When he couldn't, he moved on down the line. Sometimes Carrie followed along, trying as best she could to put together a home. More often than not, she stayed behind,

INTRODUCTION

usually in Meridian, where at least there was "family" and some semblance of order and stability. For seven hard years they shifted about, enduring the endless burdens and humiliations of poverty, sickness, and failure. Of this period, Carrie would write simply, with her characteristic stoicism: "We had our ups and downs." But it cannot have been as light and bearable as she makes it seem, and surely the weight of it wore no lighter with the warnings of family and friends ringing in her ears.

"Adversity is sometimes hard upon a man," wrote Carlyle, "but for one man who can stand prosperity there are a hundred who will stand adversity." Jimmie Rodgers, of course, took both feast and famine in stride, but it is much to Carrie's credit that she somehow handled success with as much poise and gumption as she had borne hardship. Even when he was down, Jimmie had lived—or tried to—as though he owned the world; moreover, years of "varnish haul" railroading and rambling around the country had given him an easy familiarity with the higher rungs of society, with big cities, fine hotels, expensive restaurants and other accouterments of wealth and fame. For Carrie the situation was not so simple. Somehow, practically overnight, she had to make the transition from a "weak, shy woman," as she accurately describes herself in the pre-Bristol days, accustomed to hovering in the background in shoddy apartments and cheap clothes, to the fashionable wife of a Famous Man, meeting and entertaining show business executives and celebrities, running a large household, and managing the thousand-and-one details of Jimmie's career that he was too busy or too ill to attend to. She brought it off with seeming ease, became both a grand lady and an accomplished businesswoman in the process, grew lovelier and more personable with the passing of time.

Following Rodgers's death, her life seems to have been bound up largely with two overriding concerns, that of perpetuating her husband's memory, and keeping the royalties coming in. It is only natural that the two interests often merged. To those ends she made personal appearances and maintained a voluminous correspondence with both record buyers and professional people; she sought to promote a number of singers, notably Ernest Tubb, who might record Rodgers's songs or otherwise keep current his style; ultimately she sacrificed, in all likelihood, her second marriage because, as she later said, "The fans won't let me be anything but Mrs. Jimmie Rodgers." [4] And, in 1935, in collaboration with her good friend Dorothy Hendricks, she wrote *My Husband, Jimmie Rodgers*, which for some forty years was the only full-length account of the life and musical career of a most significant figure in American cultural history. [5]

As a book, *My Husband, Jimmie Rodgers* is no less an anomaly than its author. Privately printed in the first edition, it has had a somewhat checkered career. Today, original copies are avidly sought by collectors, but it is doubtful that Mrs. Rodgers ever recovered (at $1.25 per copy, postage paid) the expenses of its publication, for country music fans do not exactly constitute a prime market for hardbound books, even biographies of their idols. Perhaps with this in mind, the book, retitled *Jimmie Rodgers' Life Story* and embellished with pictures of the principal figures, was reissued in paperback by Ernest Tubb Publications in 1953, to coincide with the first Jimmie Rodgers memorial celebration in Meridian (known then as "National Hillbilly Music Day"). Apparently even then sales were none too good, for Jim Evans later found several hundred copies stories in a Meridian garage, rescued them from mildew, and made them available to members of the Jimmie Rodgers Society. The supply was soon exhausted, and the book was essentially out of print from the early 1960s until 1975, when the CMF Press issued a third printing, a reproduction of the original text. The present edition has been completely reset, with the addition of this introduction, a chronology of Rodgers's life, illustrations, and an index.

INTRODUCTION

3

Important as *My Husband, Jimmie Rodgers* obviously is as a cultural and historical document, fans and scholars alike have complained of the book's sketchiness, its casual omission of important details, and its lush, often melodramatic tone—all those overwrought exclamations and sobbing dashes ("No money for toys! No money to buy—a little white casket"), as though Charles Dickens were being rewritten by Walter Winchell and a Hollywood hack. But of course Jimmie Rodgers himself had never flinched in the face of sentimentality, and very often he made it work, as Carrie sometimes does. Perhaps much of the fevered style may be attributed to the influence of Mrs. Hendricks, who had been an actress and obviously had a certain flair for drama.

Then, too, it helps to recall the spirit of the era in which the book was written. Life in the thirties had been reduced to its barest essentials emotionally as well as economically; at the same time, the unrelieved rigors of daily existence allowed—if not, indeed, demanded—expression of those feelings in a manner far more flamboyant and fanciful than that permitted by the ironic sense so pervasive in our cynical age. While it is unlikely that little Jimmie Rodgers ever had to beg milk for his cereal, or that he literally sang Carrie's mother away from Death's door, the remembered quality of those real or imagined events captures the essential nature of the Rodgers legend, along with such equally disingenuous but authentic details as those of little Anita's pathetic letters or Carrie's willingness to sell her winter coat to buy food. For all its bathos and effusion, *My Husband, Jimmie Rodgers* is no less a genuine expression of its author's attitudes than the blatant, often hysterical "star biographies" of our time.

More valid perhaps are the charges that the narrative is slanted and sometimes incomplete or erroneous. Despite Carrie's assertion to a potential reader some years later that the book "answers . . . any question one might have in mind about [Jimmie]," [6] many Rodgers buffs find the book, at least on first reading, something of a disappointment. There are dozens of tantalizing omissions: the dates and details of Rodgers's "med show" tours in the early twenties, the names or backgrounds of the Jimmie Rodgers Entertainers and other accompanists, accounts of how or when Jimmie composed and recorded his songs, his abortive (and not very laudable) career as "detective," the names of the towns, big and little, where he made personal appearances—all these are glossed over, in a rush, it seems, to tell "the story," to heighten, to dramatize, and thereby authenticate the legend. We are told that in the early years of their marriage, Jimmie "bought phonograph records by the ton," but nowhere do we learn their titles or the names of the artists who may have brought a gleam to the eye of "the father" of country music. Her account of the events of 1923–1926 just prior to Jimmie's big break at Bristol, and so vital to an understanding of his development—is so irregular and vague as to seem deliberate, an effort conscious or otherwise to cover Rodgers's random wanderings and their equally random separations. There is, of course, no mention of Rodgers's marriage in 1917 to Stella Kelly (a beautiful and intricate girl whose own life became almost as interesting, as adventurous, and in its own way, as tragic, as Rodgers's), nor of the daughter born to that marriage—apparently because Carrie held the notion, a misguided one as it turned out later, that Stella had designs on the Rodgers estate. For similar reasons, we are told nothing of Cora Bedell, Jimmie's private nurse, whom he platonically adored, and who accompanied him on that fateful last journey to New York.

In the face of so many missing details, however, it is important that one bear in mind the title of the book. Despite her claim that *My Husband, Jimmie Rodgers* would "answer any question one might have in mind," it was not really Carrie's intention to write a full-scale, formal biography of the famous personality billed as

INTRODUCTION

America's Blue Yodeler, but rather to portray, from her own very special vision, the common and complex man whom she knew best simply as "my husband." If the picture is blurred or occasionally blank, one recalls that the law of the land still dictates that no wife be compelled to testify against her spouse. What she more nearly accomplished, of course, is an account of her own life-and-hard-times (filtered, as one might expect, for public consumption) as wife, guardian, nurse, helpmeet, loyal fan, and ultimately, Gallant Widow, of a whimsical, erratic country genius named Jimmie Rodgers. She had, indeed, many roles to play.

There is the further circumstance that Carrie was simply not present in every instance to record the scenes and events of Rodgers's professional life. In the last years especially, he often traveled without her on tours and recording dates: moreover, many of the minute facts of his career, so desperately sought after by fans and academicians, simply did not interest her. That however does not entirely explain all of the inaccuracies and contradictions which continue to plague scrupulous historians. Some of the objections are relatively trivial, as for example the debate over when Jimmie first began to "tack on" yodels to his songs. Others fault her chronology, complaining that she incorporates certain songs into her story long before they were written, but that is easily explained as a simple misreading of the text, and of her intention. The lyrics she cites are purely for dramatic and narrative effect, a part of "poetic license" rather than any attempt to relate art to reality. On other points, she seems merely to have drawn from unreliable secondhand sources, such as newspapers or current rumors. Yet that does not account for every discrepancy. She may, for instance, have simply accepted Jimmie's version that he was "motherless at four," but that hardly explains how she could have described their sojourn in Florida as lasting "the better part of the year," when in fact it was barely five months. Her version of how Jimmie first learned that Ralph Peer was in Bristol differs substantially from other equally reliable reports, as does her entire account of that first recording session. There is also the wonderfully dramatic tale, now part of Rodgers lore, of how Jimmie, his first record hardly released, drove their old Dodge to New York with less than ten dollars in his pocket, checked into the expensive "Menger" Hotel, and called up Peer to arrange a second recording session. As a characterization of Jimmie Rodgers—audacious, full of charm, sure of his own talent, a confidence man in more happy ways than one—the story is only too apt. According to Peer, however, it was he, not Rodgers, who initiated the phone call, and their momentous second meeting came not in New York but "when [Rodgers] stepped off the train in Philadelphia." As usual, both versions have some basis in actuality, but in this instance the scale seems tipped in Carrie's favor, despite certain errors of fact.[8]

When she wanted to, Carrie could be remarkably candid, most notably when dealing with Jimmie's boundless ego and her own occasional (but quite understandable) lapses of faith. She was more than a little shaken to hear him blithely announce to a chance acquaintance, only minutes after cutting his test record, that he was "under contract to the Victor phonograph company" (in Washington a few weeks later, solely on the basis of his very brief stint at WWNC and a single, as-yet-unreleased record, he had letterheads printed proclaiming him "National Radio Artist—Victor Record Artist"), and she deftly deflates one of the more beloved legends—a story that Jimmie did not hesitate to pass on and in fact may well have originated himself—to the effect that his fame had come overnight as the result of a single radio broadcast heard by Victor officials, who dropped everything and rushed off to the hinterlands to sign him up. Interestingly enough, in laying this "fantastic tale" to rest, she offers a most telling reason for its having flourished: the principles involved "hated to spoil such a beautiful Fable by getting it all messed up with the truth." Clearly, there were other fables, some not so beautiful, which Carrie Rodgers did not want "messed up with the truth."

INTRODUCTION

4

It is not easy to explain the complex, often contradictory elements which made up the man now honored in country music as having "started it all"—perhaps such an explanation shouldn't even be attempted—but whatever else he may have been, Jimmie Rodgers was absolutely one-of-a-kind. In the first thirty years of his all-too-short life, he tried a lot of things— railroaded, drove a truck, worked as a mechanic, took several flings at show business, stoked furnaces, even ran a filling station—and failed at everything he did. He was too frail for the robust life he so desperately sought, and he wasn't even much of a musician: couldn't keep time, read a note, play the "right" chords, or write lyrics that fit. The fact is, Jimmie Rodgers was ill-suited for just about everything he tried except for touching the hearts of millions of fellow Americans, and lifting them up. We are richer and better for his having been here, and we honor him with our abiding interest in the sad, funny, and moving saga of his life and art.

If *My Husband, Jimmie Rodgers* does not immediately satisfy one's interest in the subject, it is nevertheless remarkable how very much the book gives up when one has learned the objective facts of Jimmie Rodgers's life. Perhaps those are the easiest to come by, anyway. What we really crave are the personal details: Jimmie's passion for cornbread-and-milk, Old Golds, and good old cane syrup, his yellow Ford roadster and his favorite guitars, his frustration at having his name misspelled, his unshakable optimism and his total professionalism, the great and gallant spirit with which he lived, worked, created, and died. This is the true legacy of Jimmie Rodgers, as delineated in the book now before us.

—Nolan Porterfield

NOTES

¹ In a letter to Virginia Lee Campbell, January 8, 1938.

² Bill C. Malone, *Country Music, U.S.A.*, revised edition (Austin: University of Texas Press, 1985), p. 440. See also Mike Paris and Chris Comber, *Jimmie the Kid* (London: Eddison Press, 1977), pp. 7, 55-56.

³ Although it is possible that Carrie knew Rodgers before his marriage to Stella Kelly in 1917, it seems more likely that they met in the spring or summer of 1918, after the marriage (in another part of the state) had broken up and Jimmie's rambling ways had brought him back to Meridian, where in January of that year he had gone to work for the New Orleans & Northeastern Railroad. As is often the case, Carrie is vague about the date of their meeting—perhaps deliberately so.

⁴ It seems worth noting that the sole condition of the divorce decree (1941) was the restoration of her former married name.

⁵ The first extensive biography of Rodgers was the Paris-Comber book, published in England in 1977. My biography, *Jimmie Rodgers: The Life and Times of America's Blue Yodeler*, was published by the University of Illinois Press in 1979. [*In fairness to Mr. Porterfield, it should be noted that his Rodgers biography, a landmark of country music scholarship, is generally acknowledged to be the definitive one. —Ed.*]

⁶ Letter to Virginia Lee Campbell, January 8, 1938.

⁷ The age varies from story to story; one prominent account makes him as young as two. In fact, Jimmie was almost seven when his mother died in 1903. The point is not especially significant, except that it minimizes the time during which "little" Jimmie was supposedly shuffled around between relatives and foster homes.

Actually, his childhood, up to the age of twelve or so, was reasonably stable. During much of that time, following his mother's death, he lived in the home of her maiden sister, Dora Bozeman, who upon the death of their parents had taken over the old Bozeman "home place" at Pine Springs. It was apparently a happy, convivial place; "Aunt Dora" adored Jimmie, and he reciprocated, visiting her in later years whenever he could and writing regularly from the distant places to which he roamed.

[8] For one thing, there was no "Menger" Hotel in New York—it was the Manger. But Carrie (and Jimmie) may have simply confused it with the Menger in San Antonio, one of the many Baker Hotels in Texas where Jimmie later made his headquarters. Peer's account (*Meridian Star*, May 26, 1953) is somewhat colored by his efforts to establish that he had "discovered" Jimmie Rodgers and immediately recognized his unique talent. The opposite seems more nearly accurate: until Rodgers's records began to sell in overwhelming quantities, Peer thought of him as just another hillbilly singer, with perhaps less ability than others in his "stable." A generous and generally selfless man, Peer (like Rodgers) had nevertheless read his own press notices and apparently felt, in later years, that he had historical axes to grind.

[9] See, for example, the *Southern (Railway) News Bulletin*, December, 1928, p. 3, and the *Kerrville (Texas) Mountain Sun*, April 25, 1929, p. 1—stories which Jimmie obviously had a hand in "planting."

CHRONOLOGY

of the life of Jimmie Rodgers

1897 — Born September 8 at Pine Springs, Mississippi, the son of Aaron and Eliza Rodgers.

1903 — Mother dies, probably in late autumn. Jimmie, with his older brothers Walter and Talmage, goes to live for a short while with his father's relatives at Scooba, Mississippi, and Geiger, Alabama.

1904 — October 20, Aaron marries Ida Smith, a Pine Springs widow, moves to outskirts of Meridian, a few miles away.

1905–1911 — At odds with his stepmother, returns with his brother Tal to Pine Springs to live with relatives of their mother.

1911 — April, wins amateur talent contest in Meridian, leaves town with a traveling medicine show. A month later, quits the troupe because, as he writes to his Aunt Dora Bozeman, "the show man wound [sic] treat me Right." Takes job with a clothing merchant in West Blocton, Alabama. In December, is "retrieved" by his father and put to work as a railroad section hand on the Mobile & Ohio Railroad.

1912 — August, in Artesia, Mississippi, suffers severe illness, is put to bed with chills and symptoms of pneumonia.

1913–1916 — Works at various railroad jobs around the state; in June 1916 goes to Texas seeking work but returns to Mississippi.

CHRONOLOGY

1917 — May 1, marries Stella Kelly, daughter of a Winston County, Mississippi, farmer.

1918 — January 9, employed as brakeman by the New Orleans & Northeastern Railroad on passenger runs between New Orleans and Meridian. February 16, daughter Kathryn born.

1919 — In November, separated from Stella Kelly.

1920 — Works for the Vicksburg, Shreveport & Pacific Railroad on runs through Louisiana. April 7, marries Carrie Williamson.

1921 — January 30, daughter Anita born.

1923 — Tries out with Billy Terrell's Comedians, tours with the show for two months. June 20, daughter June Rebecca born (dies December 22).

1924 — Roams the South and West as a "boomer" brakeman and occasional entertainer, picking up work wherever he can. Returns to Meridian in the fall with a bad cold which develops into pneumonia. Tuberculosis is diagnosed; he spends three months in King's Daughters Hospital in Meridian.

1925 — January, quits the New Orleans & Northeastern with a letter of recommendation which indicates that he is "going West" for his health, but in September he is in Florida, where he finds work with the Florida East Coast Railroad.

1926 — February, leaves Florida, possibly for Arizona and a job with the Southern Pacific. By fall he is back in Meridian, where for a short time he runs a filling station.

1927— January, moves to Asheville, North Carolina, for his health. Works as city detective, janitor, and part-time musician. May–June, broadcasts over WWNC, Asheville. In June, plays at Kiwanis Carnival in Johnson City, Tennessee, where he meets Jack and Claude Grant and Jack Pierce, forms the Jimmie Rodgers Entertainers. August 4, cuts test record for Victor in

CHRONOLOGY

Bristol, Tennessee, moves to Washington, D.C., where he plays local theaters and club dates. October 7, "Soldier's Sweetheart" and "Sleep Baby Sleep" released. In November, goes to Camden, New Jersey, for second recording session (four sides, including "T for Texas" and "Away Out on the Mountain").

1928 — February, becomes "Monday Nite Feature" on WTFF, Washington; returns to Camden where he records "Treasures Untold," "In the Jailhouse Now," and six others; records there again in June. In July, goes cruising up the Potomac on Gene Austin's yacht, *Blue Heaven*. August, appears as "Special Added Attraction" at the Earle Theater, Washington's finest. Autumn, plays the Loew Vaudeville Circuit through the South and Southeast; records "Waiting for a Train" and three others, October 20–22, in Atlanta.

1929 — January–March, tours with the Paul English Players, taking time out in February for a recording session in New York. In April, vacations in Kerrville, Texas, decides to build a permanent home there. In June, headlines the opening bill of the new Majestic Theater in San Antonio, and embarks upon a nine-weeks tour of the Keith-Orpheum-Interstate Circuit in Texas, Oklahoma, and the South. Holds recording sessions in Dallas (August and October), New Orleans, and Atlanta (both in November); travels to Camden in September to film *The Singing Brakeman*, a fifteen-minute short for Columbia-Victor Gems. Spends Christmas in his new Kerrville home, "Blue Yodeler's Paradise."

1930 — March-June, tours with Swain's Hollywood Follies through Louisiana, Texas, Arkansas, and Oklahoma, during which time he accidentally encounters Stella and is reunited with his daughter Kathryn, now twelve. May 24, meets Pawnee Bill (Major Gordon W. Lillie) and is guest of honor at his famous trading post at Pawnee, Oklahoma. Travels to Hollywood, where he records fourteen new tunes between June 30 and July 17. Meets his favorite movie stars, Laurel & Hardy, and discusses plans never consummated because of his health—for making films. Returns to Texas for personal appearances in September and October; spends the remainder of the year relaxing and resting at Kerrville.

1931 — January, stars with Will Rogers in a Red Cross sponsored tour for the relief of drought and Depression victims in Texas and Oklahoma, returns at month's end to San Antonio to record, among others, "T.B. Blues" and "Jimmie the Kid." In February, is made an honorary Texas Ranger at ceremonies in Austin; appears as featured attraction at the Texas Rotary Clubs statewide convention in March. June, in Louisville, Kentucky, to record eleven numbers, including three with the Carter Family. November, sells "Blue Yodeler's Paradise" and moves to San Antonio. Meets Will Rogers again and is guest of honor at Rogers's birthday party. Joins Leslie E. Kell Shows for appearances in Houston and San Antonio.

1932 — January 19, begins twice-weekly program on KMAC, San Antonio. Records in Dallas, February 2–6, and in Camden, August 10–29. Tours briefly with J. Doug Morgan Shows and makes sporadic personal appearances on his own, as health permits. October, travels to Meridian for Golden Wedding Anniversary of his wife's parents.

1933 — January, health deteriorates rapidly; enters Baptist Hospital in Houston. In February, returns to San Antonio, with orders to rest; instead he travels to Paducah, Kentucky, to help his old friend Billy Terrell, whose show is suffering from the Depression. In May, goes to New York by steamer from Galveston, accompanied by his private nurse, Cora Bedell. Records twelve numbers, May 17–24. Dies, May 26, in his suite at the Taft Hotel in New York. Buried in Oak Grove Cemetery, near Meridian.

(Compiled by Nolan Porterfield)

CHAPTER ONE

"The cares of the day—

"Slip softly away—

"When I hear-the old home call—."

The first time my husband, Jimmie Rodgers, mentioned "his book" to me, he had been idly strumming his beloved guitar and, in a low voice, singing a phrase or two now and then from my favorite, "The Home Call."

Presently he said: "Mother, they keep after me to write a book." Surprised, I looked up at him. But I didn't smile. He went on: "The story of my life." And he gave me a quick look—expecting to discover me highly amused—and was plainly relieved to see I was smiling, not derisively, but with real pleasure.

I said instantly: "Jimmie! Why don't you? Really I think you ought to."

That pleased him. "Honest? Shucks, though: I don't know anything about how to even start writin' a book."

"But, darling; no one would expect you to turn out to be a regular author. You could just tell your story in your own way, couldn't you? Just write it all out—same as you tell things to me."

My husband said doubtfully: "Well-I—aw, shucks, I don't think it would be so hot." Then, with mounting enthusiasm, he added: "At that, though, I've had some funny experiences, maybe. Been a lot of places. Met some pretty well-known folks. And—I've won recognition."

Recognition! When for five years and more the RCA Victor Company had

1

been steadily acclaiming Jimmie Rodgers, "the singing brakeman," America's Blue Yodeler, as their greatest star. But then—Jimmie Rodgers was—different. He sang of, to and for the underdog—the forgotten man.

But, that day my Jimmie must have had a premonition that he'd never get his book written, because he said to me: "If—if anything happens, Mother, so I don't get it written, you be sure and write it—will you, Sugar?"

I gasped and protested: "Jimmie! Why—I couldn't." Unthinkingly then, I used his very words. "Why—I wouldn't know how to even start writing a book."

Jimmie laughed and quoted me in return: "No one would expect you to turn out a regular author. Just write it out in your own words, couldn't you?" His voice dropped then to a tone of earnest pleading. "Promise? Promise me you'll try anyway, Carrie?"

I nodded slowly. "I'll—try, darling."

So—I'm doing the best I can, now, to keep that promise; to tell the story of his life; his humble boyhood and carefree early youth; his cheerful Irish stubbornness in refusing to let poverty or sorrow or heartbreaking disappointments spell defeat. And—his gay defiance of his enemy, "that old T B."

Jimmie's book! It would be so much more interesting if he could just be here beside me—to tell me what to say. Almost, I can see him glowing with pardonable pride over some remembered honor. Grinning, chuckling over some amusing incident. And I can see his small-boy delight in little things that pleased him.

Memories. Crowding so fast they confuse me. His teasing "yodel-ay-ee-whoo-whoo-oo—." His constant longing for and interest in the life of the railroads, the silver rails, old smokies. And he so loved pretty train whistles!

I still have his voice—"The Home Call" and the others. Haunting melody. Silvertoned voice. The magic strumming of his old guitar.

Quite vividly, here beside me once more, I see my Jimmie lounging comfortably,

MY HUSBAND, JIMMIE RODGERS

brown eyes half closed, singing softly and lazily caressing that famous guitar. In his eyes, in his voice, that yearning tenderness, that heartfelt devotion to home and family.

"In the evening—just Carrie—Anita—an'—me—."

CHAPTER TWO

"You tried hard to bring me up right—"

The owner of the restaurant peered down at the wistful-faced youngster climbing up onto one of the high round stools at the long counter.

"Please, Mister—would ya gimme some milk in a bowl? I got my own corn flakes."

Repressing his amusement, the owner asked solemnly: "Got any money—for the milk?"

The boy looked up, earnest pleading in his brown eyes. "Mister—I mean—will ya jus' gimme it?" He repeated impressively: "I got my own corn flakes."

As the over-large bowl of milk was set before him, small Jimmie Rodgers busied himself opening his treasure—a sample package of cereal swiped from some unsuspecting housewife's front porch.

Box-car homes or railroad boarding houses failed to furnish the kind of food a growing boy needs, so small Jimmie Rodgers foraged for himself. He watched for and followed after those wonderful men who, in kindly fashion, went about distributing manna. With small-boy cunning he managed to snatch many a sample carton of cereal from many a front porch. But cereal needs cream; or, anyway, milk. Little Jimmie Rodgers found the way. Almost every proprietor of lunchroom, cafe or restaurant adjacent to "the railroad yards" heard that wistful appeal: "Mister would ya gimme some milk in a bowl?" An appeal that was always answered—usually

4

with rich cream. His was a familiar little figure in and around "the yards." He was known to be the son of a section-foreman on the Mobile & Ohio Railroad: Aaron W. Rodgers' boy.

Many youngsters, spending the years of their boyhood as Jimmie did, would have been forlorn, lonely little humans. But little Jimmie Rodgers, with his Irish heart and wistful charm, took life as he found it; and found it good. Left motherless at four, with scarcely anybody but a too busy father to note or care where or with what companions the boy spent his time, Jimmie managed to make of his boyhood one long Great Adventure.

There were thrilling rides on switch-engines; rides still more thrilling on the tops of lurching box cars with indulgent "real-for-sure" brakemen. He could climb up or be lifted into the cab of a great black monster, and be permitted to pull the cord, his childish ears delighted with those dearly-loved whistles. He could lounge in switch-shanties with "rough and rowdy," but kindly railroad men, listening to—and learning—ballads of the rails and even barroom ditties.

But the father, Aaron Rodgers, must be given full credit for doing the best he could, with but limited time and means, to provide for his motherless children. Small Jimmie and his much older brothers, and later a younger sister. There was for a time a step-mother, but when she died little Jimmie was, once more, left without a woman's guiding hand. There were "visits" with relatives in small Alabama or Mississippi towns.

I believe it was in the village of Scooba, in Mississippi, that Jimmie had—to use George Cohan's words concerning his own early life—"the only smattering of real boyhood" he ever knew. There he scrambled over the lime rock hills, up and down the steep banks of the "crick," hunted chestnuts and scaly barks, and dug his toes into the sand when questioned too closely about some boyish prank.

An aunt of his once missed a half-dozen or so of her best sheets. Jimmie was also missing. When found they were, of course, together; but—"several towns away." Jimmie was owner, manager and chief actor of his first tent show. His aunt's sheets, tacked and nailed to any sort of post or tree, were doing splendid duty as "the big top." They were now useless for home purposes—but Jimmie insisted he'd made enough money to buy dozens and dozens more "old sheets."

CHAPTER THREE

"Hey, little water-boy,

"Bring that water 'round;

"If you don't like your job

"Set that water-bucket down—."

Fifty cents a day, all his own, must seem riches to any small boy—unless he's a baby movie star.

The grinning, hard-working blacks who took Aaron Rodgers' orders made his small son laugh—often. Though small he was white. So, even when they bade him "bring that water 'round" they were deferential. During the noon dinner-rests, they taught him to plunk melody from banjo and guitar. They taught him darkey songs; moaning chants and crooning lullabies.

Those days he didn't try to sing much. His voice was too uncertain.

He liked hearing himself sing; but, being modest and easily embarrassed, he preferred to avoid the danger of ridicule.

Therefore he listened while the darkey section laborers twanged their banjos and sang. Perhaps that is where he leamed that peculiar caressing slurring of such simple words as "snow"—"go"—so that, in later years when he crooned to the world:—"been away too long, up with the ice and snow-oo, somehow I crave to travel back where the warm, warm breezes blow-oo" listeners in far-away lonely shacks were enthralled.

When Jimmie Rodgers quit his summer job and returned to school Aaron Rodgers opened a charge account in a large department store.

MY HUSBAND, JIMMIE RODGERS

This, he felt, was necessary now that Jimmie was back in school and living in a railroad boarding house while he, the father, must often be too far away, working some distant section, to see that his boy had clothing, shoes or school supplies that he needed.

To Jimmie this was a splendid arrangement. It offered vast possibilities. To his small-boy mind it meant that the store man was a good friend of his father's and was kind and generous enough to give gladly anything from his shelves which Aaron Rodgers' son might desire. Just what good were those things doing anybody, anyway, lying up there on the shelves or hanging from the racks?

Immediately Jimmie possessed himself of a brand-new suit; blue—his favorite color. Another little boy, a schoolmate, fingered longingly an olive green suit, Jimmie didn't think so much of that. But—the next day he returned to the store, alone. If the clerk was surprised when Jimmie demanded that the green suit be boxed for him, he said nothing. He had his orders.

By night Jimmie was two dollars richer; and Aaron Rodgers, without knowing it, had been charged with another eight dollars. This, for Jimmie, was a beautiful scheme. There were jack-knives in the store, roller skates, "B-B" guns, and hats and shoes for boys.

So, for a time, Jimmie "earned" a nice, easy dollar or two every few days. He could see all the picture-shows—which about then were spreading so rapidly in popularity—and he could march right into any restaurant and have a grand meal. Also, he could have all the chocolate creams he could possibly eat, but there's no fun eating chocolate creams all by yourself. No fun in having fun of any kind—all by yourself. Jimmie never enjoyed anything unless he could share it.

Then, looking around for more worlds to conquer—in the store—he discovered the camping-goods section. This led to the grandest idea of all.

Once again little Jimmie Rodgers disappeared. When found, he was "several counties away"—with his second tent show! And making money!

But a certain department store had Aaron Rodgers charged up with an expensive khaki camping tent; the largest and finest in the entire stock.

This, of course, ended a small boy's dreams of a sort of Santa Claus store, the owner of which was, as he had thought, a close personal friend of his dad's.

CHAPTER FOUR

"I'll eat my breakfast here—

"And my dinner in New Orleans—."

The railroad yards! They were "home" to the section foreman's little boy.

Powerful black monsters belching fire and smoke; smoke white, chiffon-blue, blue-black; smoke shot through with crimson and gold. The cheery rattle and clank of gaily drunk box cars and flats. The jauntily curt "whoo-whoo"! as the "hoghead"—perhaps small Jimmie's favorite engineer, acknowledged the yard-conductor's signaling arm.

Steel rails often slippery with rain, ice, fog, dew—but always silver. The crunch of cinders. The smelly whiff of creosoted ties. Hurrying figures. Lounging figures. Men "rough and rowdy"; but men with jovial, weathered faces and great generous hearts. Men in stout blue overalls and jackets; tight peaked caps on their heads.

Gray heads, black, red, bald, brown. Men with blue bandanas knotted around their leathery necks. Each man wearing the inevitable trainman's "watch and chain."

Great engines puffing, snorting; suddenly spitting out hot steam. Great steel hearts throbbing with eagerness to be heading out; or sighing contentedly, their day's work done, as they headed in.

Too, there were arrogant Pullman trains flashing on to distant, glamorous cities. Or creeping along carefully—humbly obeying the signals of some lowly blue-garbed figure; or—dusty and weary—submitting gratefully to the clean-up gang; the repair crew.

MY HUSBAND, JIMMIE RODGERS

Small Jimmie Rodgers loved it all. The hurrying noisy days. Magically colorful, throbbing nights. And always, throughout the yards, men in blue tapping their shoulders, jerking their thumbs, whirling their arms, beating their fists together—or slapping their middles.

If at night, lanterns swinging in half-arcs, grand full arcs; jiggling smartly up and down, or slowly sidewise. Signals!

At fourteen, the small son of Aaron Rodgers knew them all; knew every signal of this queer deaf and dumb language. At fourteen he could laugh gleefully right along with the oldsters, at the new brakie high on a box car, alert for relayed signals, who suddenly twisted the wheel and called out eagerly: "Go eat. O.K. Suits me fine!" Jimmie knew as well as the most experienced trainman that the relayed signal, two smart slaps on the head-brakeman's middle, meant they were heading for track eleven.

At fourteen Jimmie knew the rule-book better than some preachers know their Bible; although it is doubtful if he had ever, up to that time, seen even the outside cover of the rule-book. Still, Jimmie knew all the answers. When a fireman asked him: "What makes up a train crew, Jimmie?" the boy answered readily, brown eyes twinkling:

"Hoghead, swellhead, two empty heads and a baked head," which slang of the yards meant engineer, fireman, two brakemen and the conductor. On occasion he would, just as readily, refer to the conductor as "the brains," and to the fireman as "the tallow pot."

He could repeat, and laugh at, the greenhorn brakie's definition of a "fixed signal." "A brakeman on top of a box car, dark night, lights out—and a cinder in his eye."

Long after he was forced to give up railroading because of failing health, when we'd be driving somewhere alone and neared a street signal, Jimmie would hark back to his railroad days, and call out alertly, if weakly: "Yaller board, Mother"—"red board" or "clear board—step on it." Then, at fourteen, or thereabouts, Jimmie Rodgers became, to his huge delight, a real-for-sure railroad man; assistant foreman to his father.

Shortly afterward he got a job as a real brakeman! His first job was on a work train, but very soon his older brother Walter, already long in the service of the rails, got him on as a regular on the New Orleans and Northeastern, from Meridian to New Orleans.

He had by then lost his baby chubbiness and was stretching upward, becoming a tall, husky young fellow. Long since his baby curls had turned to rich dark brown.

His railroad card shows fourteen years of service. During those years he played various roles on many roads; call-boy, flagman, baggage-master, brakeman.

Flagging passenger trains gave him a chance to wear a neat uniform. Always meticulous about his personal appearance, his erect bearing delighted his bosses. Nearly always it was Jimmie who was called when some very special train was due; a train bearing officials of the road, or some notable—like General Pershing.

But—"I crave to cover distance"—so, as freight brakeman, young Jimmie Rodgers thought he was doing fine. He was going places, seeing things, doing things. Carefree, happy always, when answering a call he reached first for banjo, mandolin or ukelele. When he wasn't "riding the decks" singing, testing his lungs against the rumbling, swaying box cars, he spent his time in the waycar plinking darkey melodies to admiring crew buddies. He didn't suspect, then, that often those older men deliberately shifted many of his duties to their own shoulders, thus leaving the young brakie free to plink away to his heart's content—and their delight.

His voice was full-throated now; but his singing no better, perhaps, than the average young fellow's. But he was gaining confidence. The crews heartily enjoyed his rollicking ballads of the railroads, his plaintive crooning of plantation melodies, songs of hills and rivers, as well as countless barroom ditties. He was railroad man— and minstrel. And the war was on and troop trains were being rushed madly here, there, everywhere.

It has been said that he answered his country's call during those terrifying times of 1917–1918 by serving in the navy. Jimmie Rodgers served his country by doing what was required of all railroad men; by attending to his trainman's duties. For the railroads had requested the goverment to exempt all trainmen.

Full crews, experienced railroaders were sorely needed to work troop trains and long trains of supplies and equipment being rushed to ports and training camps. It was impressed on the minds of all trainmen that theirs was a highly important branch of the army. So Jimmie Rodgers did his bit by "going high" on the tops of lurching box cars in sun, wind, rain, sleet, snow; by relaying signals, twisting the wheel, pulling pins; helping speed Uncle Sam's trains on their way.

And a pal of Jimmie's, Sammy Williams, told his sweetheart goodbye and went to France—to be killed in action.

So before the war was over Jimmie found time to pick out words and air to his first composition, a sentimental song. If grammar, punctuation and spelling were faulty—tenderness and emotion were not. When the world heard this first song of Jimmie's the world approved in no uncertain manner; even though there was in it no hint of what would later be called "his sentimental ballads which trail off into a mournful yodel."

From the first his railroad buddies liked the song, and the young fellows in Meridian who were his boon companions liked it. With banjo, guitar, uke, they hung around the all-night places or strolled the streets playing and singing Jimmie's song along with "Sweet Adeline" and other sentimental ballads.

But it was not until some ten years later that the world heard—and approved of it.

"He said good-bye little darling—to France I must go—they took him away to this awful German war—The third one wrote by his captain—My darling dear was dead—But I keep all his letters—I'll keep his gold ring too—."

CHAPTER FIVE

"Our hearts will be so light—
"While we wander there tonight—
"Underneath the Mississippi moon—."

A school girl, a minister's daughter, I was not thinking of young men, nor of marriage. My lessons and my church and Sunday school work were to me not dull, but happy, enjoyable duties. Ours was a religious family; but none of your stern, sour fanatics. Ours was a happy home with good clean fun; with good music, the classics and popular music, as well as church songs.

To this home, then, an intimate family friend, a young lady, brought one evening a stranger, a young railroad man. And never, never shall I forget the painful embarrassment that meeting brought me! What young girl wouldn't be embarrassed, meeting a personable young stranger for the first time, looking the scarecrow I did that night!

I suppose it may seem incredible that a self-assured, likable, good-looking young man who'd "been around" could have his interest caught, even for one moment, by a church-going homebody girl still going to school; especially as she was certainly anything but prepossessing in appearance when he first laid eyes on her! Crumpled kitchen gingham; hair slicked back into a tight knot; face red and swollen from vigorous rubbing and thickly plastered with cold cream—to say nothing of gobs of the greasy white cream oozing through her fingers.

At home—the home of my parents, Rev. and Mrs. J. T. Williamson—we had a telephone and a piano. That night the family friend, bringing with her a strange young man, came barging in, without knocking or other announcement of her coming, as was her way; intent on the use of the telephone and the piano. For, as always, Jimmie Rodgers was easily persuaded to go whenever there was music to be enjoyed—even to a minister's house.

Two of my older sisters were quite "musical." One of them played in church and for various lodge and other gatherings. She was then teaching her younger sister, Elsie, all that she herself knew about music, and how to make readable copy in "notes and bars," of their own compositions. Some ten years later Elsie was to receive an urgent summons from her brother-in-law, Jimmie Rodgers, to come to his assistance; to collaborate with him. For, as he said: "I don't know one note from another." Consequently, he had to have some "write out" his songs for him, words and music. Also, many of Elsie's own appealing little songs of the heart Jimmie Rodgers later made famous.

So, this night the young brakeman was shyly glad to be admitted to our house where there was a piano and stacks and stacks of sheet music, dozens of song books, containing all the quaint, old-fashioned songs he loved, and which he could roam through at will—hymn-books and all. But when, unannounced, he had hesitatingly followed our friend through the front door and into our living-room, no one was there. But the door to the front bedroom adjoining stood open, the room was bright-ly lighted—and before the dresser-mirror stood Rev. and Mrs. Williamson's seventh child, Carrie Cecil, industriously plowing cold cream into her face!

I had just finished the kitchen work and was hurrying to get at my lessons. None of us expected callers that night. Before I realized it, our friend and a young strange man were staring in at me—laughing and teasing. Both of them, as Jimmie would have said, "were dressed fit to kill," for they were planning to go on to a concert.

There was I, so mortified I could have bawled—and no escape. I'd been taught to be polite to "company"; make them welcome. So—nothing to do except make my excuses as soon as possible—and hurry to clean up a bit; fluff my hair and climb out of that house dress into my pretty blue crepe. Then to rejoin the group now around the piano. And steal embarrassed glances at the good-looking stranger. Our "company" stayed so long, enjoying this impromptu concert, that they were somewhat late for the professional concert.

It would seem that I was fated to make the worst impressions possible on my future husband! The very next time he saw me I was parading around through the house—being "cute." As usual, when no callers were expected, I was in kitchen gingham, hair pulled back. Always, those days, rather shy in the presence of strangers, I was bold enough with home folks. When one of my older brothers complained of his new shoes being too tight, I said: "Give 'em to me. I'll wear 'em."

Into the living room I went, stumbling along in a pair of new black shoes, masculine shoes which appeared to me, gazing down at them gleefully, about the size of box cars. And there came a polite knock at the front door!

Nobody but myself in the front of the house! Timidly I pulled open the door, hiding behind it as best I could; and there stood Jimmie Rodgers, all dressed up, freshly barbered and shined, banjo under his arm, his hat in one hand and a package which any girl in the world would know was a box of candy in the other.

I had to admit him. Further, although he pretended he had expected to meet the "family friend" who had brought him to our house a few nights before, some way he made it plain that it was really my school-girl self he had come to see.

Again some member of the family came to my aid, and confusedly I excused myself, once more to get "cleaned up" in my favorite blue crepe—for this good-looking young railroad man who played the banjo and sang: "He said good-bye little darling—to France I must go—."

CHAPTER SIX

"When it's peach-pickin' time in Georgia—

"It's gal-pickin' time for me—."

Naturally, being the type I was, I was worried a lot about "my fellow's" care-free ways. In fact, I'm afraid I wanted to make him over.

"Jimmie," I pleaded. "Why don't you quit running around? You ought to be more steady; quit throwing your money away; when you come in from a run, go to bed and sleep—instead of parading the streets, serenading all the time."

Jimmie protested: "Aw, shucks, Carrie, what's money for, what's life for, if you can't enjoy 'em? I want to live—today. That old eight-wheeler might take a notion to leap the rails—tomorra!"

The very thought made me gasp: "Jimmie!"

Jimmie grinned, as usual. "Don't you worry 'bout me, kid."

"Well, I do! Everybody's saying you'll never amount to anything. That you'll come to no good."

To that Jimmie Rodgers gave the same answer eager young fellows, with their full manhood years ahead of them, have given since time began.

"I'll show 'em! I'll amount to something—someday."

"Passenger conductor?" I asked hopefully. "Well—have to wait on seniority for that. I don't know what. But I'll make good. I'll show 'em." And he added wistfully: "Anyway, how'm I hurtin' anybody with my playin' and singin'?"

17

"Well-I, nobody, maybe, but yourself. You know you ought to get more rest. And be saving your money."

"Why should I? What for? You won't marry me."

"But, my goodness, Jimmie. I'm still going to school!"

"You could quit school.—You won't even give me a kiss."

There we were; back to the same old argument!

I've been taught that a nice girl wouldn't kiss any boy or man—other than a relative—unless she was definitely engaged to him. Neither would a nice girl telephone a young man unless she had an urgent and very definite reason for doing so. And most certainly a nice girl would not dream of visiting a young man in his bedroom. Yet—Jimmie Rodgers was the cause of my breaking those rules—all three of them.

I'd admitted that I cared for him and expected, in some distant future, to be his wife; but I wouldn't engage myself to him—and I was firm in my refusal to give him even one kiss, until one night I had a bright idea. If he would give me his promise to go to church, I'd give him—one kiss. He got the kiss; and kept his promise—by going to church at least once!

Then, one Sunday evening a pal of Jimmie's kidded him: "Just saw your girl up on the corner, talkin' to a good-lookin' red-headed guy."

Jimmie grinned: "No, ya didn't. I just come from puttin' her on the street car. She's goin' to church."

But his pal convinced him, at last, that he was telling the truth. And—he was. Poor Jimmie was so hurt and miserable he failed to keep his next date with me or even telephone and ask for "the little girl in blue." And I didn't know why; didn't know what it was all about. And of course I wouldn't consider phoning him to find out. Our romance would have been broken on the rocks of suspicion and jealousy then and there, I suppose, if Jimmie hadn't decided to unload part of his troubles on my girl friend.

MY HUSBAND, JIMMIE RODGERS

Nice girl or not, bold or not, I rushed straight to the telephone to do a lot of frantic explaining. A lot was needed, too! Jimmie Rodgers had put two girls on the street car that Sunday evening; myself and my girl friend. We had not gone two blocks when she caught sight of that "good-lookin' red-headed guy." Perhaps she had some explaining of her own to do. Anyway, she insisted that we get off that car, saying we could catch the next one—and that she'd pay my fare. So, because a certain "good-lookin' red-headed guy" just happened to be lounging on that particular corner at that particular moment, I almost lost my Jimmie.

And the time I broke the most inflexible nice-girl rule by visiting him in his bedroom—.

But something else, just as important, must be told first.

In the fall and winter of 1919 the flu again swept the country as it had in 1918. Doctors, nurses, anyone who was well enough to get around, were on duty night and day. Almost every family had at least one dangerously sick member to be cared for; some of them had three or four, at once.

In our family we had two; my mother and one of my sisters were both in grave danger; Mother especially. As it happened, I was the only one at home at the time to care for them; give them their medicine, prepare broth, attend to their needs and wants. To make it easier for me to wait on them both they had been placed in separate beds in one large room. Mother was weakening rapidly—because of loss of sleep. For more than three days and nights she never closed her eyes in restful sleep.

For more than three weeks I had not been outside of the house, night or day; had scarcely changed my clothes. Slept in snatches. And—Jimmie Rodgers had the nerve to call me up and ask if he could come by, with his pals, at 2:30 in the morning, when he got in from his run, and serenade us!

The idea was preposterous, and I told him so. But—and I could almost see him hunching closer to the phone in his eagerness to make me understand—he insisted:

"Listen, Carrie, we'll play and sing real soft and low. And if it bothers them you can motion from the window—and we'll go right on away. You know, sometimes music soothes—if it's low and sweet."

"Well-I—all right, then, but I know they won't like the noise. And if Mother has managed to get to sleep—and you wake her up—." I couldn't finish. If that happened I couldn't imagine what the result might be. Still, perhaps he was right. Maybe it would help make the painful hours pass—and I was hungry for the sight of him; even his dim shadow seen through the window in the night.

They were there—playing so softly that I'd hardly been aware when they first started. Mother and Sister seemed to be resting as easily as I could hope for under the circumstances. So I slipped outside, to stand by Jimmie just for a moment. The low music went on. I was sure it wouldn't bother Mother and Sister—because I was sure they couldn't even hear it. Then I thanked the boys, told them they'd better leave, and hurried back into the house while they were still playing.

And—in the big bedroom Sister was making frantic motions at me! I thought she meant for me to call the doctor quick—that Mother was dying! I wheeled to run to the phone, but Sister hissed at me: "No—no! She's asleep. The music put her to sleep! Tell them to keep on. Don't let them go away."

But it was too late. Already the soft, sweet music was withdrawing into the night—and Mother was sleeping as peacefully as a healthy child. For long hours she slept, and when she awoke we knew that all danger was past.

And she said: "I had such a beautiful dream. An angel choir—playing the sweetest, softest music for me. Until I woke up I didn't know it was a dream. I thought it was real."

"It was real, Mother," I told her. "That was Jimmie Rodgers and his friends."

Mother was thoughtful for a moment; then she said solemnly: "If that was Jimmie Rodgers he saved my life. God bless him!"

MY HUSBAND, JIMMIE RODGERS

My precious mother is still living as I write this in 1935. And I thank God that He put it into my Jimmie's heart to insist on that serenade in 1919. Jimmie knew, better than I, the magic music can weave.

But it was not long after—in the following spring—that Jimmie had a long siege of pneumonia. And when I couldn't stand it any longer, nice girl or not, I went to his bedroom to see him, taking a girl friend with me. He was getting better; still, I was a little surprised when we found him not only sitting up—but dressed, and trying on a new pair of shoes. He'd just received a long delayed paycheck and had ordered several pairs sent over for him to select from. That he was glad to see me was evident in his suppressed excitement.

Finally, when the other girl's back was turned for a moment, Jimmie made wild motions to me. In pantomime he held up his right hand as for a vow; then quickly pretended to slip a wedding ring on the third finger of his left hand; all the time nodding at me vigorously, smiling wistfully, eagerly.

I nodded; and then, I'm afraid—I giggled.

Our companion didn't know that a proposal had been made and accepted—during the few seconds she'd had her back turned.

But I'd decided that having Jimmie was better than school.

And Jimmie sent back all the shoes. He saved the money!

The next day, at noon, I left my schoolbooks with my friend and hurried downtown to meet Jimmie in front of a department store. After assuring himself that I was actually there, he said: "Wait a minute——" and hurried across the street—to a jeweler's.

He came back with my wedding ring; gold—yellow gold. He thought those thin white gold circlets didn't "look married"—and he wanted this job done right.

The ring he'd bought, without even letting me help select it—or see if it fit—was a perfect fit.

MY HUSBAND, JIMMIE RODGERS

Jimmie always said that I cost him eighteen dollars. That's what he paid for the license, the ring—and the preacher.

So—at 12:30, noon, on the seventh of April, in the year 1920, we were married by the Rev. J. L. Sells, in Meridian, Mississippi.

We caught the first train for New Orleans for our runaway honeymoon of three days; and the little new bride who was Mrs. Jimmie Rodgers had not even one suitcase or piece of luggage of any kind! "We'll have a long honeymoon and settle down for life—."

But it seemed we were never to get settled down—and we could have only three days to enjoy our honeymoon all by ourselves because all we had with which to face the world were the few clothes we had—and forty dollars in cash—all that was left of Jimmie's check after "buying" me.

Of that forty, immediately after the ceremony he gave me half; twenty dollars. And from that day on, all throughout our life together, he gave me half of every penny he earned—whether it was two dollars, thirty or a thousand.

"We'll travel through life in a hurry—sharing the good and the bad."

CHAPTER SEVEN

"In one-horse town or city—

"No matter where we are—

"I'm happy if I have you with me—."

So that was the Jimmie Rodgers I fell in love with and married; the Jimmie who was a brakeman, a nobody; a happy-go-lucky youngster forever strumming and singing—when he wasn't "going high" on box cars; caring little whether he had a job or not—but loving the old smokies, silver rails and the hollow whistles from "that old smokestack."

Whistles? Pretty train whistles? Well—I was pretty indignant about that matter on occasion—until I understood him better. He'd jump up from the table, leaving a delicious, nourishing hot meal to grow cold and tasteless—while he rushed outside where he could hear better, to—listen; just listen to some old smokie in the distance—"whoo-o-who-o-o—."

While we'd been going together he'd never been in the least worried about getting a job—or keeping on. Laid off? Fired? No matter. "I went to the depot and looked up on the boa'd—I says it's good times here—but it's better down the road—." Or maybe it would be a rollicking: "I'm Alabama bound—with a banjo on my knee—."

But—now! He had himself a wife. And—jobs were getting scarcer and scarcer. But my young brakie husband never lost courage. His spirit, his heels, were just as eagerly confident.

As for me, of course I was thankful whenever he had a call, a job; even when it meant that gay "Throw your things together, kid. We're leaving here for there." Very soon I learned to keep my things thrown together; and not to question why. I might be a home-body girl, longing to just stay put; be settled in some little place of our own—but: "Throw your things together, kid." It was that—or be left behind. So—it was that.

Gaily we'd leave here for there—although often there'd be no sign of a job waiting for us. But—made him no never mind. He'd get one. "I will, Sugar. You just wait. I will."

But—a job meant going high, swinging to iron ladders. It meant—well, we need-ed the money, but with me now was the constant fear every railroad man's wife must know. If one of those powerful eight-wheelers left the rails—.

We didn't have much trouble adjusting our married selves; much less than is usu-al, I think. Of course, to me my young brakie seemed just about perfect. But nat-urally, our personal habits were some different. I'd had a home. My boy had little knowledge of any home except railroad boarding houses. For all that, he was so sweet about trying. And if I'd find myself just a little put out about something, I had only to remind myself: "Shame on you. He loves a home; even when it's only a one-room light housekeeping home. He's taking care of you, loving you—and he keeps you laughing. All you've got to do is make him happy."

But—he certainly did have some astonishing ways! For example, long after I'd be asleep he'd rouse me to plead: "Look, Sugar. Help me remember this, will you? Were you asleep? Gosh, I'm sorry. But look! I just figured out a rattling good title for a song—and I'm afraid I'll forget it 'fore daylight. Help me remember it, will you?"

I'd try—but so often when morning came, neither of us could remember. I saw to it then that every night before we extinguished the light there'd be a pencil and tablet handy on a chair by my pillow. Sometimes I merely reached over and scrawled his dandy little title or idea in the dark. But if he'd composed several verses lying there in the dark before he called me, then we'd light the lamp and, while he kept busy remembering, I'd jot them down. Some of these got lost through the years, but others we preserved and they certainly proved worth the keeping—to say nothing of our trouble and loss of sleep.

I remember that he roused me one night to say: "Listen, Hon. You remember me talkin' about So-and-so quite a lot? Well—poor devil—his wife run off with another guy week ago. I just heard about it. Sure makes me feel bad. She—she took his kid; cute little tike; little girl, just three years old. Poor devil! He's just all broke up about it—."

And that night was born another song destined to become famous.

Yet, as I drifted back to sleep I knew only that my singing brakie was worrying about another little song of sadness out of that sympathetic heart of his; another minstrel lay, another tender little ballad of a broken heart.

So, I knew, had "Soldier's Sweetheart" been composed. So, I knew, would be many another. To what purpose? None, it seemed. Yet, simply because they were there in that Irish soul of his, they would give him no rest until he could give them to God's whole world in song.

Together, then for seven years, we had our ups and downs; our downs and ups.

Chicken one day; feathers the next, but it seemed that our chickens were mostly all feathers—like a screech-owl.

Still, even when things looked most gloomy, we would cheer each other up by discussing our great ambition—an impossible ambition it seemed, despite Jimmie's stout assurance that—some day—he would bring it to fruition.

We would stand in front of that wonderful show window down town, often going blocks out of our way in order to reach it, and gaze longingly at the shining new Buick displayed inside. We thought then that we'd never want anything else in the world as we wanted that Buick.

"Just you wait, Sugar. I'm going to buy us one, just like that—some day."

MY HUSBAND, JIMMIE RODGERS

"Blue, Jimmie," I would remind him, to which he would agree: "Sure. Blue's the only color there is. Blue—to match your eyes."

Later, when we became proud parents, he always called me "Mother," and in the family circle always spoke of himself as "Daddy." But whenever he said "Carrie" in his southern drawl, it came something like "Cara." Being Southern myself, I'd never noticed it.

But in later years a friend asked Jimmie if he knew that "cara" was a Latin word, meaning "beloved." He didn't, of course, but after that he often took particular pains to call me "Cara," his eyes twinkling—but affectionate intent clear. However, when he used my name in any of his song-numbers, for the sake of rhythm he made of my name two very distinct syllables: "Car-ree."

CHAPTER EIGHT

"Not a nickel in my pocket—

"Not a penny can I show—."

When the little water-boy collected his fifty cents a day I am reasonably sure he spent at least fifty-five of it; and when the happily confident young brakeman earned thirty dollars a week he easily found ways of spending thirty-five. He always declared that money was no good until after you'd spent it; then it was good, for it had furnished you and those around you with the good things of life—and had gone on to do the same for others.

Before we were married Jimmie laughed indulgently at my repeated attempts to get him to save his money. As I told him, his spendthriftiness worried me, especially when he tossed his money away—receiving for it nothing but a good time or perhaps some useless gewgaws, such as those silly trophies he would load himself up with on a carnival midway. But Jimmie protested: "Gosh! Those show folks are human, same as us. They gotta live. Ever think of that?"

From the beginning, it seems, Jimmie Rodgers was fascinated by shows and show people. Most growing boys—and girls—are, but some of them get over it. When Jimmie haunted the show lots and the stage entrances of theaters he dreamed, as other boys have, of the time when could strut about those stages, those lots—as one of those wonderful beings. With adult years he put the dream aside, happy in how own work on the rails; until his strength was no longer equal to twisting wheels and pulling pins.

27

MY HUSBAND, JIMMIE RODGERS

After marriage I stopped trying to make Jimmie over. I loved him; the Jimmie he was—not the sober-souled Jimmie he would have become if constantly nagged. When he had money and wanted to spend it, I was glad to see him getting pleasure out of doing so. When I could, I saved the half of his earnings which he never failed to give me. And gaily—when he wanted me to, and he usually did—I helped him have fun in spending his. His pockets all had holes in them; any money that went into them went right on out again. In later years, the same. When gold rolled in, it joyously rolled on out. Which is the reason why we never tucked away the millions popularly supposed to have been ours. As he said once: "If you're happy-go-lucky you'll be happy-come-lucky, 'cause luck will come to you."

But it seemed, sometimes, that luck would never come—to us.

The last of January, '21, Jimmie got the first work he had been able to get for a long, long time. But he didn't want to leave me for even one hour. We needed money desperately just then—for an impending and most important event. I told him not to worry. I'd be all right and he'd be back in plenty of time.

Up the line somewhere, on his very first run, he received a message telling him the glad news. His baby daughter, Carrie Anita, golden-haired, blue-eyed, had arrived safely. Under like circumstances I think most newly-made fathers would have worn a wide grin—and kept right on working. No so Jimmie Rodgers. He found a substitute to relieve him and caught the first passenger train back home.

And why Carrie Anita? Well, Jimmie and may others had long insisted that I looked so much like Anita Stewart, then such a well-loved screen star, that Anita should have been my name. Both Jimmie and I had always been crazy about Anita Stewart.

During our New Orleans honeymoon Anita Stewart had been on a personal appearance tour; so we actually had a chance to see her! I'm not quite sure, but I think she did a song number with yodeling.

MY HUSBAND, JIMMIE RODGERS

Anyway, it was so pleasing; so different from the blarney, blasty yodeling so many were doing—or trying to do—at about that time.

Therefore, because we both thought Anita such a pretty name, and because we both admired Anita Stewart so greatly, Anita was added to my name in that of our first daughter.

It was two years later, in June, that our second baby, June Rebecca, with dark hair and eyes and olive coloring like her Daddy's, came to join the struggling little family.

Young Jimmie Rodgers now had a wife and two baby daughters to support—when he was scarcely able to support himself. Happily confident, he would trail jobs here and there.

CHAPTER NINE

"But in my checkered life I find—

"Nothing comes right—it seems—."

Coming in from his run shortly before daylight one morning, my boy found a distressed member of the family anxiously awaiting him at the station.

His golden-haired, two-year-old, Nita, was dying—of diphtheria.

Jimmie came—white, shaking, terrified—to find neighbors, relatives, two doctors and myself waiting; just waiting—.

The two doctors had, they said, done everything that man could do. No one but God could save her now, they told me. So—I pleaded with God: "Dear God—please! You don't need her, do you? You can't need her as much as we do! Please let us keep her—But—if—it—be Thy—will—."

Jimmie's arms were around me; for an instant only. He went to his baby; then turned quickly to stare in scorn at those solemn-faced humans waiting there—helpless—while our precious Nita lay battling for breath, for life. He flung out at us all: "I'll give her some medicine that'll cure her!" and went hurrying to the kitchen; leaving a horrified group around the little bed.

"Jimmie!—Jimmie—What are you doing?" I ran to him, unable to believe my eyes. He was frantically mixing a hot toddy of "nigger gin"—to give a helpless baby! A baby—dying—.

He ignored shocked protests; ignored my wild pleadings. The doctors drew

30

back. Their attitude said plainly that, as the child was near death, anyway—well, if the grief of the frantic young father could be lessened by thinking he was doing something—anything—.

In an instant, it seemed, the miracle happened; the phlegm broke!

And as I'm writing this I hear my healthy, happy girl calling: "Mother. O, Mother!"

But—if it had not been for Jimmie and his bottle of nigger gin—and God who put it into Jimmie's heart to ignore us all that day!

Christmas season of that same year found Jimmie Rodgers walking the streets of New Orleans—jobless. The railroads were firing; not hiring. His stomach was empty; his shoes needed patching; he was shabby. Long since he'd sold, traded or pawned his few stringed instruments; banjo, mandolin, ukulele. He had left his guitar at home. Those days he seldom strummed a guitar; preferred the others, it seemed.

Christmas season and no money. The thought of going back to Meridian without a penny, without a little gift for his wife, toys for his babies, was almost unbearable. Still—he could be with them. The Yuletide wouldn't be quite so cheerless if our little family of four could spend it together.

So—in the Meridian yards he crawled off a freight—to find some one waiting for him—hunting for him.

Someone who told him that his littlest baby, June, was dead!

The message we thought he had received had failed to reach the forlorn wanderer.

No money for toys! No money to buy—a little white casket.

Loyal, kind-hearted relatives paid for everything. He would get work again—some time. He would repay them. But—that black hour came near crushing that dauntless spirit forever; near—but not quite.

Is it sacrilegious for me to wonder—if resourceful Jimmie had arrived in time—? But I hadn't wanted to add to his worries. I hadn't realized the danger—until it was too late.

Out of cigar boxes Jimmie carved little toys for Nita; a little trinket box for me; and then for himself, he made a ukulele. And he amused our one little toddler with rollicking songs—in a voice which clutched at my heart; a voice plaintive, sobbing, appealing—in spite of its effort to attain a lilting gaiety.

We both rejoiced when his name went up again on the extra board. Work again! A "stake"! We could pay debts; could have some of the things we'd had to do without. But—it was winter time; and his call was to far-western railroads; Colorado, Utah. Our little Nita was too precious to risk such hardships. So Jimmie didn't, this time, command me gaily: "Throw your things together, kid."

Alone, he hurried on his way—to the work that meant so much to us; and came home several months later with another bad cold and an ominous cough which he made light of, but which terrified me.

"Shucks, just a cold, Honey. I'll be okay. Don't you worry."

But—the cough hung on—and flecks of blood appeared—and then came the only hemorrhage he had ever had; but it nearly took his life that autumn of '24.

For three months my boy lay there, in a charity hospital, fighting for his life. It was four miles from my mother's house. I had no car; sometimes no bus fare. But I managed, some way, to get out there every single day; sun, rain, sleet or snow, whether I could get a ride or was obliged to walk. My Jimmie had told me he couldn't stand it if he didn't see me every day.

You see, we both thought—we were afraid—."

So—when he was released from the hospital after those three agonizing months— we knew. Knew that never again should he be a ladder climber; never again ride the decks and test his lungs against roaring winds and clattering empties; never again collect a railroader's stake.

So they said.

MY HUSBAND, JIMMIE RODGERS

Too, they ordered: "Higher altitude. Plenty of sun and fresh air, but no exposure to rain and cold. Do nothing to cause physical exhaustion."

That to a railroad man, a brakeman, without a dime to his name—with a wife and child. That to a man who was untrained, unskilled in any other kind of work. Never ride the decks again, nor strum banjo in the waycar with his crew-buddies gathered around him.

Well—orders or no orders—Jimmie Rodgers did! But not for a time; not until he really thought he was well enough. For a time he did his best to obey the orders of the "T B" doctors. He had to get well, he said, so he could make a living for his little family.

He strummed his cigar box ukulele and crooned quaint, old-fashioned lullabies to Nita playing around his feet; and sang again: "For the soldier who was so true—." And wept slow tears because it was Christmas again—and no money for little Nita's toys.

And was ashamed and hurt because I worked as an extra sales-lady during the Christmas rush—so that Santa Claus wouldn't quite forget our baby. But I told him gay little stories of the crowds and confusion in the big store—and told him he couldn't expect to be strong enough to stand heavy work—just yet.

I tried to persuade him, too, that the doctors were wrong: "Maybe there was a spot—started there in your lungs, Honey; but I bet it's gone by now. Why, you're actually getting fat."

He knew I was storying; and I knew that he knew it. But—it was much nicer to pretend, I thought. And then I heard him moaning, in song—song that had an impish note: "My good gal's tryin' to make a fool outa me—tryin' to make me believe—ain't got that old T B."

But while that impish, mournful chant went on my husband was evidently doing a lot of thinking; pondering, wondering—what next? He told me, grinning: "Just tryin' to catch up with my worries, Mother. But don't you worry. We'll come out of it okay."

Oftener now he would pick up his little-used guitar. Some way it seemed to suit his mood better these days.

"We'll travel the road together—leading to lands afar—no matter what the weather—strummin' my old guitar—."

CHAPTER TEN

"T for Texas—

"T for Tennessee—."

The mountains? Fresh air and sunshine? No exposure to cold winds and rains? No physical exhaustion?

Fine—but who was going to pay the bills while he battled that "old T B"? He had to work. He was sure he could work. Now that he'd had care, treatment and rest he felt as strong and well as ever—almost.

Still, we both realized too well the presence of that terrifying specter waiting—just waiting–.

He had to be doing something, for the sake of his eager soul as well as for the sake of his loved ones. He refused to be downed. Jimmie Rodgers, the singing brakeman "temporarily" on the "off list," did not hesitate to clutch bravely, gratefully, the opportunity whimsical Fate now dangled before him. He smeared greasy black stuff on his face, snatched up the banjo provided for him, stood on street corners and strummed and sang, while nasal voices roared out: "Another bottle, Doc."

Blackface entertainer for a "physic" show! Pagliacci in cork!

If my heart was as heavy as I thought of my beloved wandering throughout Kentucky and Tennessee with a shabby little medicine show, singing to guffawing groups, though even appreciative groups, in crossroads villages, nevertheless I told myself: "He's happy—thinking that now he's able to support us even if he has got—tuberculosis. And he's able to have, too, all the things the doctors told him it was necessary for him to have."

Jimmie sent me his salary—so pitifully small every week; every cent except his living expenses. And I, saying nothing, put it away—every cent of it. For I was doing now what Jimmie would never give me permission to do; holding down a steady job, earning sufficient for my own and our little daughter's needs.

Cheery, happy-hearted letters came—one each day. "Feeling fine. Gaining weight; sleeping like a top." But—I could still hear in memory that daring, gay, mournful: "Got that old T B—I can't eat a bite—Got me worried so—I can't even sleep at night."

But Jimmie's small-boy dreams had come true! He was "an actor"! If the reality lacked glamor, at least he was getting, that summer, not merely the lucky chance to obey the orders of the T B doctors—while being paid for it—but also valuable professional experience. He was gaining confidence—under that mask of black; ease, "stage presence." Too, he was making valuable contacts; meeting on intimate terms other musicians, professional even though itinerant. All that—with a shabby little "med-show," but it laid the groundwork for Jimmie Rodgers' future; it revealed to him the way to his "alley"—even though the way seemed often dim and uncertain.

And the grandest result of that summer's wandering through the mountains of Kentucky and Tennessee was that, apparently, he had actually licked that old T B!

He had left the med-show in mid-summer to join another street-show, a novelty attraction making larger towns. He was a white-face entertainer now, and getting a better salary. He wrote me that he thought it was a money-maker and that he would like to buy an interest in it—if I could get along with a little less while he was paying it out. Of course, I told him: "Go ahead. Fine."

His judgment proved good. He made money, bought the owners out. Continued making money; proud owner and manager of his own road attraction! He would "enlarge"; he would buy out an Hawaiian show with a carnival. Into that went his all, his summer's work and profits, aside from what he had sent me.

And immediately hilariously, tornadic winds laid the carnival in ruins and swept away young Jimmie Rodgers' "roll"! He came home—flat broke.

Flat broke—but happily confident. "Never mind, Mother; we may be down—but we're not out. Wait'll I go down to the yards. I'll find a job. They tell me the roads in Florida are begging for good men."

"Jimmie! Not—not railroading—again!"

"Shucks, Honey, why not? What else can I do? The show business is no good, winters. Anyway, don't you worry. I'm okay now, sure nuff."

Flat broke, but light-hearted. And suddenly he sat, strangely quiet, looking down at his cupped hands—while slow tears came. For into his hands I had stuffed money; every cent he had been mailing to me week after week, all summer long.

And then I told him. About my work at the newsstand down at the Union Station, on the night shift. And I said to him gaily: "Don't you dare cry! And don't you dare grouch at me, either, Jimmie Rodgers! 'Cause Honey, I knew I wouldn't be quite so lonesome, wouldn't have time to miss you quite so much, if I had work to think about."

After a long moment he said brokenly: "I don't know what I've ever done—that the Master up there—is so good to me."

Then he reached for his old guitar and told me, in song: "Whenever I'm up you are near me—giving me happiness—and when I'm down you cheer me—nothing could be better than this."

CHAPTER ELEVEN

"—from now on, when writing me—

"If not there, just forward, please—

"Somewhere below the Dixon Line—."

Miami. Bright blue skies. Deep blue waters. Caressing, sunshiny winds. Palms. Orange groves. Excited, hurrying crowds; boom crowds.

And a boomer brakie, lithe-bodied, bronze-faced, in blue bandana and watch and chain, again riding the decks, testing his lungs against the clatter of lurching box cars, his ears again hearing that beloved "bark of the old smoke-stack"; happy because his little family, his wife and adored four-year-old, were there too, making a gay little home out of a shabby little apartment; happy because of his "stake" that was steady and sure.

But with me—once again—was that haunting fear: If that old smoky leaps the rails—.

I have heard Jimmie mention railroad wrecks but infrequently; and then only hesitantly, moodily. He was never in a serious wreck of any kind. But there were times when auto drivers failed to hear or see roaring, oncoming trains speeding through the night, or around hidden curves. It seemed he couldn't speak of them; broken bodies pitifully quiet; the screams of human beings, men, women and children in agony.

In his songs he told often of troubles, sickness, of being broke; but he never had a morbid tale to tell; never a recital of horrors. "Ben Dewberry's Final Run," one of his well-liked recorded numbers, tells of a fearless engineer killed in a wreck, but it was not one of Jimmie's own compositions. He liked to sing it, though, in tribute to the memory of his favorite engineer, Jim Jackson, who was killed in a wreck. I know that Jimmie grieved for him as only a man can grieve over the loss of a well-loved friend.

In Miami, then, Jimmie worked steadily for the Florida East Coast Railroad for the better part of a year—and we saved our money!

Together we'd had some bitter lessons about the empty pockets business. So we saved. Just the same, our knuckles were to be again rapped smartly, over and over. But at the moment we had a nice little roll.

"Throw your things together, kid. We're going home—for a visit with the folks."

"Jimmie! You get—fired?"

He may have been storying, but he told me: "Nope. Quit." He grinned—and then sobered. "Truth is Mother, I—I reckon we better head for Arizona. Southern Arizona. Don't worry, though. I'll get another good job out there. I know a fella in Tucson—."

So—after all, he hadn't licked that old T B! Soft, moist breezes, however alluring, can be deadly to diseased lungs. He had tried to keep me from knowing; had tried, I think, to keep himself from knowing. He had kept up his gay spirits and had seemed so strong and active. But—that ominous cough. It was back, constantly growing more ominous. I didn't know much about such things, and he had laughed at my worries. "Shucks, Mother, just caught a little cold." But—now—.

Now, we told each other, we'd find health and happiness—and a job—in far-away Arizona.

If Jimmie's thoughts turned longingly to the show-business at this time he didn't mention it to me. His last experience had been rather disastrous, financially. And our little family had, it seemed, to be torn apart for one reason or another, too often as things were.

Somewhere—probably at the bottom of a dump heap—is the very first car we ever bought, a little second-hand Dodge. Gaily we loaded onto it our early possessions—in grips, suitcases, packages and bundles—and my little trunk.

"Here we go—just we three—O, how happy we will be—."

We weren't happy, telling the home-folks goodbye; but we were young, we were together, and we had money! Such a lot of money, we thought.

Westward we drove; and Jimmie tried out his first yodeling to amuse himself and us as we rode along and we decided it was pretty good. He held his lively youngster, our adored Anita, on his lap and let her "drive." And he "blew train whistles" with his throat—and raced trains to give "the boys in the cab" the on-the-spot signal, laughing to see them stare.

Arizona. Altitude. Healing dry air. But these are of little use when accompanied by physical exhaustion and worries.

The Southern Pacific yards in Tucson are known to all experienced railroad men as being about the toughest spot—for a brakeman—in the United States. Mountainous box cars plunging down steep hills require strong bodies, arms of steel, powerful chests on the men who must control them. Twisting wheels is not enough; brakemen must use what is called the "brake stick." This requires more strength, more endurance than a sick boy with wasting away lungs can furnish.

Gamely, almost angrily, Jimmie Rodgers clung to that job. For—here we were, almost a thousand miles away from home—and our pockets empty again; our beloved little car sold "to live on."

Jimmie refused flatly to let me try to find work. It would have been difficult, among strangers, but I wanted to try.

Grimly enduring the torture of his work one day, my poor boy would be bed-fast the next, his strength completely gone, his body in agony, his flesh dry and burning hot with fever. Rapidly, surely, he was killing himself.

I told him so, and I pleaded. "Darling! Think of us. Suppose you hang on unnecessarily until our baby and I might lose you!" "But, Carrie, what else can we do? We got to live! Don't you worry, kid. I'll be okay—in a few days. Just got to get used to this climate. Anyway, Mother, we can't get home—on nothing."

"Well, let's go as far as we can! And you can get work where it won't be so hard; where you won't have to fight the brake stick."

He fought against the idea. He had a job. We needed the money. He wouldn't be a quitter. But when I made him think it was for our sakes, not his, that I was asking it, he finally agreed: "Mebbe you're right, Mother. We'll see. Try it another month, anyway."

Another month—and there would be, I was sure, only two of us left in that far-away land.

The next night Jimmie came home weak, exhausted, but grinning. He told me, with his old gaiety: "Throw your things together, kid. We're taking the first train for Texas. Got passes gettin' themselves fixed up, Texas! Whoopee!"

Already he was better—at the very thought of heading homeward! And of being freed from that torturing brake stick. That night, for the first time in weeks, he picked up his old guitar and while I hurried about packing and Nita lisped over and over: "Goin' back see G'amma'," Jimmie sang banteringly "T for Texas" and caroled again the yodels we'd decided were pretty good. And again "blew train whistles" with his throat. We couldn't suspect then that he was to make them both famous.

We couldn't hope to get all the way back to Meridian—to spend Christmas with the home folks. Jimmie said he'd take the first job he could find along the line. Might get one in San Antonio.

Foolishly, gaily we spent our few dollars for a Pullman berth, for meals in the diner—and for tips! And for Nita and me Jimmie strummed his guitar and sang softly. None of our neighbors seemed to mind.

The Pullman conductor, a genial white-haired man, came often to sit with us and there was talk of railroad men and prospects for better times—railroad times. And he seemed to enjoy hugely Jimmie's railroad ballads.

Presently Jimmie and his guitar and a group of men were somewhere in the rear—and there was laughter; and I smiled, knowing my young husband was giving them some of his "rough and rowdy" stuff. I knew, too, that he was feeling better, was stronger and happier than he'd been for a long time; because we were heading back to Dixie, because for an hour or so he could forget that old T B that nearly had him down; nearly—not quite.

On this trip it might have saddened him a little if he had known that, already, he had done his last railroading.

At the Sunset Station in San Antonio the three of us, tired but happy, crawled off that eastbound train, strangers in a strange city. We hurried across the way to the nearest little hotel, engaged a room for the night—and Jimmie Rodgers planked down gaily the last dollar we had in the world!

Up in the room, our little daughter already asleep on the bed, we looked at each other. We knew that, for breakfast, there were three dimes in Nita's little bank. Then—what?

As usual, Jimmie picked up his guitar; strummed idly a moment and then told me, with that whimsical, wistful smile: "I'm a broke brakie, Ma."

I asked him: "Well, what of it? We can wire the folks."

"Not on your tintype! I'll get a job—tomorra sure. My old guitar's itchin' to go see Uncle, anyway. We'll eat. Don't worry."

He knew I wasn't worrying, except about his lungs. My Jimmie could always manage, some way, to find a way out. But—I made up my mind that beloved guitar of his shouldn't go see Uncle. My little trunk was still over in the baggage room. First thing in the morning I'd get into it. There were quite a few things I could do without—and my light coat would do me. I could sell my winter coat.

MY HUSBAND, JIMMIE RODGERS

In the morning we found my trunk had gone places. Been carried on down the line somewhere; Galveston, perhaps.

And—nothing for my brakeman husband in San Antonio. I knew that Jimmie Rodgers would do most anything before he'd whine to another railroad man for a loan. Jimmie was a boomer brakeman and proud of it. A boomer, temporarily jobless and with stomach empty, will slap another railroader on the back, saying: "Hello, Bill, how about a feed?" And will accept, as a matter of course, the meal set before him, but he disdains to ask for cash. Although his own fist is always ready to dig instantly for another's need.

Jimmie said that morning: "Goin' out for a while, Mother. Goin' to make the rounds. Be back, couple hours, maybe. And don't you worry, Sugar. Just trust me."

When he came back he had two one-dollar bills. To me they looked like two one-hundred dollar bills. He said: "Found out about a job in Galveston, so we'll just trail along after your trunk."

The two dollars? I don't know. He told me he'd run across a "guy" whom, years before, he had fed and staked. Maybe so. But—he had taken his guitar with him and had brought it back. I've often wondered if he "entertained" in some poolroom or back barroom, singing bravely his rowdy songs, to provide a ready meal or two for his wife and baby.

On passes we went to Galveston—to find that my little trunk had been delivered to somebody else! When the authorities finally got it back for me, we found that my "valuables" had been stolen. But—the express company paid us full value.

Then, with money in our hands, Jimmie told me: "Mother, I reckon you and the baby better go on back to Meridian. No work here, and if we just stall around, we'll live this up—then all three of us will be stranded. We've got to think of her. You two go on the train—and I'll be home almost time you are."

I could see he was right. But—leaving him sick, broke, almost a tramp? The

MY HUSBAND, JIMMIE RODGERS

Texas skies were sunny then; but it was December. A norther, a blue norther, might pounce on Texas, and my boy, so gamely resisting that old T B. My husband in want—lacking nourishing hot food, a comfortable bed, thick wool blankets for protection against the chill fogs—!

But—our little Anita was precious to us both; so finally and most reluctantly, I obeyed him, leaving him there to bum his way back to Meridian as best he could. I told him: "Just the minute I get there I'll send you some money—if only a couple of dollars. And please don't go hungry. If you need money before I get home, you wire the folks."

He said he would. I knew he wouldn't.

In the day coach I wondered: Will I ever see him again—alive? Will I ever hear again: "I could never be lonely—I could never be blue—as I go through life, if only—I have my guitar—and you."

CHAPTER TWELVE

"Carolina, now I'm coming to you—
"Just to spend the spring—."

I'd hardly reached home when a message was put into my hands. Steeling myself against whatever crushing news it might have for me, I read it. And instantly my thoughts went racing around in such mad circles I couldn't think at all. Whatever did it mean?

Mother and Dad waited; wondering, fearful. I gave them the slip of yellow paper, and together they read it. They looked at me; they looked at each other. Then, while Dad nodded gravely, Mother said: "Carrie, you're going to send that boy fifty dollars."

Near tears, I protested: "Mother, I can't send him even five."

As if I hadn't spoken, Mother repeated firmly: "You're going to send that boy fifty dollars." And Dad said gently: "We'll arrange it, Daughter." Neither of them had forgotten that serenade of Jimmie's.

They arranged about the fifty, and rushed me on my way to send it. Hurrying along I kept telling myself: "He's in jail. He's been picked up as a vag. Or else he's just plain crazy!"

Then rereading the message, trying to decide what I should say to him, terror suddenly gripped me. He'd had another hemorrhage! He was in a hospital! Why hadn't that occurred to me instantly?

Frantically now I scribbled my message, telling him to let me know, or have

45

somebody tell me the truth instantly. If he was sick, or hurt, I'd take the first train. I didn't know how I'd get there, but I'd get to him some way. Mother and Dad and Nate and the rest would arrange about another fifty, if necessary.

He had merely asked me to send him fifty, neglecting to give any reason why he wanted or needed so much all at once. No; I take that back. He hadn't asked, he'd demanded: "Send me fifty dollars!"

Word came back that he was all right. I wasn't to worry. Letter following.

And I didn't dream, until later, what an amazed, not to say astounded, Jimmie Rodgers received notice that fifty dollars was waiting for him at the address he had given me—and that almost within the hour he'd sent his demand—collect!

His message had been simply to advise me of his new address. He'd made his way a hundred miles or so eastward and just wanted to let me know where to send the "couple dollars." The "send me fifty" he'd thought I would understand was just a little secret joke to be relished between us—since neither of us had so much as a thin dime!

But—"restless heels, soaring wings." A few weeks at home, rest, good meals, the joy of seeing his beloved old Dad and brothers, and of strolling around singing and playing with his pals, had done wonders for the wandering brakeman. He was looking better, feeling better; but he wasn't strong.

I knew now that his old strength would never come back to him unless, by some miracle, that cough could be made to disappear. It seemed to me sometimes that I could actually see his strength leaving him day by day; leaving—never to come back.

Therefore, I did the best I could to preserve what strength was left to him; to keep him from exerting himself or exhausting himself in any way. Being Jimmie, however, that was difficult sometimes. Whenever I had wood or water to carry, or some heavy object to move, I tried to keep him from noticing; or waited, if I could, until he was away for an hour or so. He never "liked" housework, as some husbands seem to, but just the same, he never could sit by and watch me lift or carry a heavy load.

Then, late in January of 1927 Jimmie grew restless. He simply could not endure being idle, just loafing, even though I told him: "No reason why we can't just stay right here until warm weather comes. Then maybe you can join out with another little medicine-show. Remember how much good trouping you did that summer?"

Jimmie said: "Yeah, I know. But, doggone it, you know what it means. I like it fine; and if I had money so's I could afford it, I think I'd just like nothing better than trouping with tent or street shows, summers anyway. But—I want my two girls with me, where I am, and that kind of life would be too hard on you both. Besides, it would mean just chicken one day and feathers the next."

"But Jimmie—we don't mind feathers. And if it helped you—get your health back—."

"Shucks, I'm all right. I'm goin' to give my two girls somethin' better'n feathers to eat. Anyway, no carnivals or med-shows on the road this time of year. I got to be doin' something—now! I just heard maybe I can get on over in Asheville."

Railroading! The thought made me frantic. He just couldn't stand it, I was positive. But—I'd made up my mind to do something; something he wouldn't like at all. I didn't tell him just then. Time enough later. Nor did I voice the protests that were in my heart. I warned myself to remember: "Contentment's just about half the battle against sickness; and it's the whole battle against despair."

So, I told him that when he was sure of a job Nita and I would come to him, wherever he was.

And then I teased: "But, Jimmie Rodgers, don't you dare tell me to throw my things together until you've got a place for us."

Jimmie grinned and picked up his guitar, as I added: "Unless you get down sick, Honey."

His eyes danced at me as he crooned: "I'm leavin' you, mama—for you know you don't treat me right!"

CHAPTER THIRTEEN

"Drop me down in Caroline—

"Caroline—that would be fine—

"I know I'll find—

"Some kinfolks there of mine—."

I hoped he would get a job in Asheville. Any kind, even railroading; anything just so it wouldn't be too hard for him. Anything to keep him from worrying, to keep his spirits up, if only for a few weeks.

By then I hoped to be prepared. Even if he got a job and sent for "his two," I knew I must be prepared. I told myself: "Just any day now he'll be compelled to give up entirely. He'll fight against it to the last, but it'll lick him sure—and soon."

Yet I didn't worry about how he would get along until he landed a job. All over the southeastern states he had relatives; old friends, old pals. Kinfolks? Scads of them. His father's people, and his mother's folks, the Bozemans. So I knew he would find good meals, good warm beds, warm fires to sit by. They would be glad to see him and would enjoy his music.

I sort of wished at that time that he'd try to learn to read printed music. Then, I thought, he might land a job with some good little dance orchestra there in Meridian. Perhaps he could earn, fairly steadily, as much as thirty dollars a week.

More and more I had come to feel that we should be settled some place. Our little Anita was nearing school age. For her sake, as well as for his, we should strive for security, no matter how small. We'd get along. I could see that not much longer, if burdened with worries and constant exposure to bad weather, could he possibly keep going, no matter how bravely, how determinedly or how gaily he struggled on. I knew if he got a railroad job he couldn't hold it. Or, if he held on grimly, anyway, it would kill him, and soon.

But, I knew my Jimmie could never land a job with a professional orchestra, even if he offered to donate his services, and even though I did think him a better musician than any of them. He wasn't a sight-reader. He wasn't any kind of a reader of music. His music was "ear music," and even playing "by ear" he obeyed no rules. He had no scorn for professional or other trained musicians; on the contrary. He never thought he was good; or that almost anybody else couldn't be better. He never thought there wasn't plenty of room for improvement in his own humble brand of music. In fact, he constantly sought his own improvement.

I've mentioned how Jimmie's spendthriftiness worried me before we were married. Well, there were three things that he would spend money for, not only before our marriage but always. As long as he could possibly scare up a dollar that wasn't busy he would spend it for shows—any kind—for phonograph records and for perfume!

He loved perfume, and nearly always carried a tiny flask in his vest pocket; not caring in the least if folks wanted to consider it "funny." In the beginning I think he turned to it as a change from the smell of the railroad yards; oiled waste and gas-laden coal smoke. Later, perfume became for him a welcome relief from the iodoform and antiseptics. Therefore, he loved perfume; the more exotic the better. No odor pleased him more than a whiff of Black Narcissus.

He bought phonograph records by the ton, I believe; and long, long before he ever dared to dream that some day a record might be made of his own voice and guitar strumming.

Working tirelessly toward the betterment of his own brand of music-making, he would play those records over and over. Then he would say, displeased: "That guy ought to tone down that banjo. Got a pretty good voice, but shucks, what's the use havin' a good voice if it's all the time drowned out?" Then he would set about seeing to it that the strings of his own banjo behaved themselves properly. It wasn't easy, but he kept at it.

Other times he'd say: "Doggone! That guy's a humdinger on that mandolin, but his singin' is a pain in the neck. Too loud and whangy. 'Sides that, what's he singin' about, anyway? Can't make out a word he's sayin'."

Jimmie Rodgers knew well enough that his accent, his manner of speaking, was neither Harvard nor Yale. He was himself. His "talk" was his own and he never pretended otherwise. He "singin' speech" was exactly the same as his "loafin' on the corner" speech. But he disliked intensely listening to a singer, highbrow or lowbrow, if he couldn't "make out" every word, every syllable.

Another complaint would be voiced as follows: "That fella's got a good voice and he can sure play that harp. You can make out what he's singin' about, too. Only thing is, no way tellin' if he's feelin' bad about it—or good about it."

All these details, then, Jimmie Rodgers worked ceaselessly to attain. The just right toning down of voice and steel strings, clear articulation and being able to make others share his emotions, glad or sad. He was supremely happy when he could find a phonograph record which, he felt, met all requirements; one in which he could completely lose himself in laughter—or tears.

But that January of '27 I could see no chance for Jimmie with a professional orchestra—unless he learned to read music. He wasn't too old to learn, but I think he must have realized always that if he tried to corral the natural music in his Irish soul, tried to confine it to "bars," there would soon be no music there; the bars would become bars of steel, not ink and paper. Caging that spirit, making it obey rules, urging it to follow signs and adhere strictly to musical measures, would have crushed out of it the spontaneity, the whimsical charm that was the really vital part of that singing Irish heart of his.

MY HUSBAND, JIMMIE RODGERS

He had, then, no rules of music or speech to hinder him. Yet, when working out any composition of his own, words and music, he refused to be content until it "sounded just right." If a phrase, a measure, seemed to lack free emotional swing, he worried it to rags; and then, figuratively, sewed up the rags again until it "fit his ears."

He blandly ignored the matter of rhyming unless it "just happened." He would even change the pronunciation of a word if necessary for more pleasing rhythm.

He scorned alike context, subject sequence and all the tenses; sometimes even the genders! And plurals and singulars got themselves gaily tangled up continuously. No matter. Did it sound right? That was all that mattered to Jimmie Rodgers, minstrel. He wanted to be sure that voice and strings expressed his moods perfectly; told the stories he had to tell, whether carefree and rowdy or heart-throbbingly tender.

CHAPTER FOURTEEN

"There's friends around and—

"Even pals that I know are true—

"Still, I'm lonely, homesick and blue—."

Jimmie Rodgers had a job in Asheville. What it was I didn't know, but he wrote me that it wasn't railroading. And the same letter brought the familiar old command: "Throw your things together, kid."

He did write that he was "working for the city." On the payroll of the City of Asheville. Well—that sounded big; but it might mean anything. He might be in the sewer gang. I knew my Jimmie. If he couldn't get the job he wanted, or one he liked, he'd take what he could get and be thankful for the chance. He'd do anything, I knew, for the sake of "his two." I remembered that dark time in Geiger, when he was on the off-list and had tried driving a truck—for a dollar a day.

Anyway, I was glad it wasn't railroading; glad he wasn't going high, running along the tops of swaying box cars or crawling, from stinging cold winds or chill, soggy air, into an always too-hot or too-cold "crummy." Whatever he was doing, I hoped most earnestly that it wasn't anything that meant cruel exposure or physical exhaustion.

Jimmie met my train in Asheville, and in his voice and eyes two queerly mixed emotions were plainly evident as he told me about his new job.

He was a city detective! Jimmie Rodgers a hunter of men!

I could imagine no job which he seemed less qualified by nature to hold.

Still, Jimmie was more than grateful to his friend, Fred Jones, Chief of Detectives, who had put him on as "special officer." If he was doubtful regarding his own worth in that capacity, at least the salary enabled him to have his family with him; and it was something to tide him over until he could puzzle out a better way; a less distressing, to him, means of earning a living for us.

Regarding my own preparedness to take on the job of breadwinner for the little family of three—if need should come—I held my tongue, knowing his sensitive spirit, knowing he'd be happier thinking it was his job and that, somehow, he'd manage. When the day came—as I was sure it would—that he would be compelled to admit himself broken in health, if not in spirit, then—my surprise.

For, when he had left for Asheville I had immediately set about, with my loyal family's help, to fit myself as a stenographer; had taken a short business course, and my brother, Nate Williamson, had arranged with his partner for me to have a bit of practical experience in their law offices. I'd worked and studied hard. I knew I could hold a job if I could get one; and I'd get one somewhere.

My girl should be educated. My sick boy should be free from worries. But as long as he was apparently happy and content, as long as he had the will and wish to be out and doing, I felt I'd be doing wrong to try to prevent him. I kept reminding myself: "Contentment's about half the battle against sickness; and it's the whole battle against despair."

Therefore, I didn't let myself worry too much about him. I even tried not to notice his cough any more, for seeing my distress always worried him. He seemed to have settled down to his job as hunter of men and to be content with it. I was wrong.

It was as I had suspected from the first. His heart had been in constant revolt; and when he began to see that his job was, so to speak, a form of charity and that the City of Asheville really had no need of Jimmie Rodgers as a "special officer," he gave it up.

Now—what? Away from home; rent to pay; jobless. Would he, perhaps, decide to send "his two" back home to Meridian, while he hunted up another little med-show, smeared his face with black and again, in little mountain villages, sang to groups of hillbillies? For his own sake, his health's sake, that was exactly what I hoped he would do. He loved the hillbillies, the same as he loved the common people everywhere, whether on hill or plain, and loved to be among them and with them. And that life was the greatest restorer of health he had yet found anywhere.

I suspected, even if he didn't as yet, that his brakeman's lantern had already twinkled out of his life; and I was glad—even though I knew he'd always love and long for the joyous life of the silver rails. But—it was "thumbs up" for him now; "on the spot"; nothing to do. Never again, I was sure, would Jimmie Rodgers relay that signal; at least, not on duty as a railroad man.

Jimmie wasted no time worrying. He found for us a little furnished cabin, a rear-cottage behind a big apartment house. This he got rent-free—in return for his services as—furnace man! Winter winds, winter weather, still hung up on there in the mountains even though summer was "just around the corner." And Jimmie insisted cheerfully: "Good times are just around the corner for us, too."

But I could tell by the way he'd sit strumming and singing softly, after his furnace duties had been attended to, that he was puzzling through his problem; not really conscious at the moment whether he was favoring us with "T for Texas" or "Soldier's Sweetheart."

I knew he wasn't without hope. He began to see dimly that his railroad days were gone; that he would have to try something else. But he would not give up. Strength or no strength; good health or no, he would plow ahead gamely, even gaily, taking the best Destiny offered, until he could discover for himself just what Destiny was hiding for him in her other fist.

And I still held my tongue—secure in my own preparedness, but not wishing to hurt him with any suggestion that as a provider he was through.

"Don't you worry, Mother," he'd declare bravely. "We'll come out of it. I'll think of something. Just don't you put any wasps' nest on the table. Just good old corn pone and ribbon cane 'lasses."

Jimmie's hated wasps' nest was store bread, which I knew better than to put before him ever, if I had any way at all to fix him hot corn bread or hot biscuits.

It is hard to say which Jimmie Rodgers loved better; chocolate creams or sugar cane. We couldn't afford chocolate creams those days, but whenever sugar cane could be obtained he always managed to have it handy to peel and chew contentedly. He never could bear to pass a syrup mill without stopping.

In later years, many times when we arrived at our hotel, swank or not, Jimmie would enter lugging an armload of cane through the lobby—blandly ignoring lifted brows and amused smiles.

But there in Asheville, in spite of all the tempting, nourishing meals I could manage for him, he was getting thinner and thinner. More and more often spasms of coughing would exhaust him so that he needed longer and longer rest periods. I urged him to go to a hospital; another charity hospital, any place where he could have proper care and treatment.

But he squelched that. "Shucks, I should say not! Your body's like any other machinery. Quit usin' it, it'll rust on you."

"But, Jimmie, just for a few weeks. Remember, in Meridian, the hospital there did you so much good."

"Yeah, but I had to go then. Don't now. Anyway, I like to never got my strength back."

"But, Jimmie—."

"Nope. Gotta keep goin'. I'm not ready to quit yet. Not by a long shot."

I wanted to plead: "Jimmie, Sweetheart, please quit trying to force yourself on. Stop and rest a while. I'll take care of you."

But you can't say things like that to a proud, stubborn Mississippi boy; a boy to whom contentment, laughter and song mean life, a young husband who hurries across to a big apartment house to play nurse to a furnace, feeding it coal and relieving it of clinkers and ashes. Then hustles back to climb into his bathrobe and out of his shoes and socks, so he can toast his bare feet at the fireplace. And who finally goes into a huddle with his old guitar in the middle of the bed, and with big toe constantly awiggle, helping him keep time, gives you impishly:

"I may need clothes—I may need hat and shoes—Makes no difference what I need—I'll never sing the blues—."

CHAPTER FIFTEEN

"Will we have to work for a living—
"Or can we continue to roam?"

The above quotation is, of course, from Jimmie's hobo query about Heaven, but it is equally apt for a boy whose weakened lungs no longer permitted him to do a man's work; to ride the deck, kick the dog and twist the wheel of a box car.

Summertime, now. The furnace no longer needed attention. So, to town Jimmie would go, guitar under his arm, to "make the rounds." This meant, I knew, the railroad yards, Fred Jones' office, the music stores or the back rooms. In some, if not in all, of those places I could imagine him with an appreciative group around him, harmonizing with him perhaps, or just listening to him and urging him to play this or that; applauding, laughing.

He came home one evening to tell me, his eyes shining: "Fred Jones says I've got all the other yodelers he ever heard beat by a mile! And you just ought to see the boys' eyes pop when I train whistle!"

Then, pulling at a strand of my hair as if it were a bell cord, he train-whistled a mellow: "Whoo-whoo-oo—."

Incidentally, that was his only "whistling" accomplishment; that "natural as life" train whistle from his throat. Sometimes when I'd call our little Anita in from play she would protest, or even ignore my summons. Then Jimmie would step to the door and train whistle and she'd leave everything and everybody to come flying. The two were such laughing-together pals always. He loved watching her small, sturdy feet flinging themselves about in those delirious Charleston gyrations, while he tried to obey her commands: "Faster, Daddy. Play faster!"

Jimmie was "tacking yodels" onto just about everything these days. Even his share of the conversation around the house was largely yodels! Perhaps you have noticed, in several of his recorded numbers some of those little "surprise" yodels, often right in the middle of phrases—a sad little yodel, or may an impish one; like a friend telling you of some incident and pausing to sigh, or chuckle.

And now our lively blue-eyed, golden-haired Anita, our little half-past-six-year-old, proceeded to spill some beans. For some moments, one morning, she had been unusually quiet, eyeing Jimmie as he worked intently on some new composition. Presently he laid his guitar aside, drew her close with a little laugh and asked: "What's my Baybo thinking about, that she's so solemn?"

"Just watching you make little curleycues with your throat, Daddy. I know! Just like Mother makes with her pencil!" She gasped, turned startled eyes to me and said: "O, Mother! I forgot!"

Like a flash then she was gone; outdoors.

He knew now, but I said lamely: "I just took a short business course, Sweetheart."

For a long moment he had nothing to say, but at last he spoke: "Maybe you're right. I haven't a thing put aside for you—in case—I—. Yes, I suppose you ought to be prepared—for her sake."

The hurt in his voice made me desperate. I protested: "But, Jimmie, it isn't only that! I get so restless—times when you're away from me so long. I feel better working. You didn't mind when I worked before—that summer you trouped."

"I would have—if I'd known. Lucky you did, I guess; and it was fine of you. Only, if you hadn't given me that money when I came home broke—I'd have figured out something. Trust me, Carrie. I'll make good yet!"

And there was nothing I could say to that but a stout: "Of course you will, Jimmie!" And then vanish to the kitchen to cry a little, in secret; tears of sympathy for, and pride in, my brave boy; with a few tears of glad relief because now he knew. Knew all about the only secret of any importance I'd ever had from him—or was ever to have.

But—he followed me to the kitchen and caught me crying. I could hear the "grin" in his voice as he said: "Whoa! What's the matter now? You go ahead, Sugar; make all the funny little curleycues you want to with your pencil, at home. I'll go on making funny little curleycues with my throat—abroad. Together, maybe we'll make out some way. You see, Mother, I figure that my yodels are going to make our living for us—or starve us to death. And we're not going to starve."

He didn't tell me, just then, what plans he had made, if any. But I couldn't see how his yodeling could possibly make a living for us, no matter how its haunting sweetness lingered in my ears long after he'd left the house. But—I did as he asked me to do. I trusted him to find his alley.

Anyway, I told myself, now that the ice is broken maybe he won't be so stubborn about accepting his wife as a working partner in the firm of Jimmie Rodgers and Family.

Sometimes—not always—Jimmie would wait to get his plans clear in his own mind before explaining them to me, but always he asked my advice before making any final decision. We had been living up—with alarming speed, I felt—the few dollars we'd been able to save that spring, but I was glad to see that Jimmie wasn't worried; though evidently he had something on his mind.

Finally, he told me: "Mother, I'm trying to pick up a couple musicians to work with me. I'd like to find a couple of nice-looking single boys—not too highbrow—who can play my kind of stuff, and play it the way I want it played. Boys who'll be willing to work whatever date I can get—schoolhouse, barn dance, road house, beer-joint—anything. Be lucky if we make our expenses for a while. But here's what I figure. Folks everywhere are gettin' kind of tired of all this Black Bottom—Charleston—jazz music junk.

"They tell me the radio stations keep gettin' more and more calls for old-fashioned songs. 'Yearning,' 'Forgotten'—things like that, and even the old plantation melodies. Well, I'm ready with 'em. See? I know all the old river ballads and—O, you know. I don't expect to set the world afire, exactly, but those, with my yodeling—and I've got some new ideas for songs, too, in the back of my head—when I get 'em worked out—."

Radio! Of course! No reason why he couldn't, I thought, even if he wasn't a trained musician, a professional artist.

But I asked: "Why not go on your own? You don't need any one to play and sing with you."

Jimmie smiled at that. "I might get scared—or run out of breath. Anyway, my long suit right now is the banjo; and it isn't so hot, solo. Not with pathetics. But I'm gonna make that old guitar of mine obey me yet—so it'll talk when I talk, and cry or laugh when I do. Think we can make out a while longer, until I get a little hillbilly string orchestra together—and working smooth—and a good spot on some radio program?"

"Of course we can. But listen, Jimmie! You can't work with regular musicians. You can't read music."

"Shucks, Mother. Didn't you hear me say I'd get the kind that was willin' to play my way? All I want's music that sounds right. I can't be bothered worryin' about playin' those crazy little fly specks with funny tails to 'em."

So The Jimmie Rodgers Entertainers were soon rehearsing like mad—in our little sitting room. And, woman-like, I began to vision my Jimmie's name in big black type right alongside The Two Black Crows. But they were comedians! Well—Caruso.

MY HUSBAND, JIMMIE RODGERS

But he was highbrow. Gene Austin? His voice was sweet—and his songs—. But no, with a sinking heart I had to admit my Jimmie was—different. Just as good—but different.

He was happy; confident, I am sure, that he had really found his alley; the alley that would soon, surely, become a good smooth street paved with gold. So near, now—if somebody didn't raise a block in his way. The block was to be raised—in Bristol. But Jimmie Rodgers tore it down.

CHAPTER SIXTEEN

"Standin' on the corner—

"I didn't mean no harm—

"Along came a policeman—

"He took me by the arm—."

And along came the Chief of Detectives and took young Jimmie Rodgers by the arm—to tell him that everything was all set for The Jimmie Rodgers Entertainers to go on the air! For the Asheville Chamber of Commerce, advertising The Land of the Sky, broadcasting from the new radio station WWNC—Wonderful Western North Carolina. Jimmie had wished, hoped, longed for that chance!

He ran hurrying home to tell me; caught me close and whispered the grand news in my ear. The grand news which nobody, of course, except the young ex-brakeman, his wife and little girl, considered in the least exciting.

Still, I couldn't help being a bit disappointed when Jimmie told me they were donating their services. I thought radio artists got paid for their broadcasts—and paid well. It sort of put my Jimmie in the cheap, unwanted class. It might mean a career for him, but not if he was willing to give his talent away. They'd expect it of him all the time, I feared. But Jimmie proved his shrewdness, his foresight, as always. As he told me: "Shucks, Mother. If I had it I'd be willing to pay 'em for this chance to get heard. Rather than lose it, I mean. Maybe there'll be enough folks listenin' in that like my kind of music to make 'em see I'm worth keepin' on. Then they'll give me a spot on the regular program. See? · That'll mean a steady salary and I'll only have to work a few minutes each day. That'll give me a chance to pick up some money outside, playin' club dates, maybe. Be easier to book dates, too, when I'm known as a popular radio artist.

Jimmie wasn't building air castles. He wasn't bragging. He stated all this matter-of-factly, as a·purely business proposition; figuring ahead as to what he might reasonably expect—and no more—if given half a chance to "get over."

He said: "Why, look, Carrie. Other fellas are gettin' by that way. Why can't I? Only I won't be satisfied with just gettin' by. If they give me a chance I'm goin' to give them my best—and keep workin' to improve that."

And he was going to have his chance! My husband, Jimmie Rodgers, a radio artist! Actually going on the air that—to us—historical night in May, 1927. Of course listeners-in would like him. And he'd be signed up immediately for a spot on the daily program. Sponsors would grab him, pester him, plead with him for his name on the dotted line. A salary, steady and sure, for just a few minutes each day doing what he loved to do; singing and strumming banjo, ukulele or guitar.

Jimmie called his little organization privately a "hillbilly ork." Well, the little hillbilly ork would make a name for itself, with my Jimmies name featured as the leader and as a sweet, yodeling singer of quaint river songs, plantation melodies and old-fashioned ballads. All these things I thought, and back of my thoughts was the knowledge that all this would mean freedom from hard work and from worries for my boy with his pitiful cough.

So my thoughts soared high while The Jimmie Rodgers Entertainers rehearsed. From my retreat in the kitchen I could hear Jimmie insisting: "Listen, fellas. Let's put more feelin' in this. This kind of stuff oughtn't to be circus-ed. It's gotta have pathos. Make folks feel it—like we do, but we gotta have the feelin' ourselves first. This is supposed to be pathetic."

Suddenly my winging thoughts crashed, kerplunk. Pathetic! Thats what folks would say of his efforts. Listeners-in would be bored; they'd swing their dials; cut him off.

MY HUSBAND, JIMMIE RODGERS

They didn't want those quaint old-timey things like "Sleep, Baby, Sleep." Goodness. That had been done for ages. Folks wanted lively, up-to-now stuff.

I was even doubtful about his "T for Texas," although it might be termed lively. Still, what in the world would people think if he sang over the radio "I'm goin' to shoot poor Thelma, just to see her jump and fall"? It certainly wasn't what anybody could call refined—but there could be no doubt of its being "different." Maybe his yodeling would put him over, if folks would listen in long enough to hear it. Still, everybody was disgusted with yodeling; blasty, blarey stuff. But his was different. If they'd just listen. Just give him a fair chance.

Thus, in Asheville, before that first broadcast, I told myself: "He'll either make good in a big way; or he'll do what he calls a complete flop." Even while I was assuring him of my certainty that he'd make good, and telling him a merry: "Good luck, darling," I was terrified at the thought the tuners-in might laugh at him. Laugh—and turn the dial.

How could they know—or why should they care—that he was a desperate, but not despairing young family man who was fighting T B? And who was depending so eagerly and hopefully on their approval for a pitiful measure of success and happiness?

It was characteristic of Jimmie Rodgers always to be happily confident of the success of any new venture. Once he'd decided it was worthwhile, he fully expected the best. But if, when he took the step, he found himself face to face with failure, he lost no time in being sorry for himself. He might be surprised, and puzzled, but he kept his sense of humor. He'd make the best of the situation while hurrying on a still hunt for a way out. You can't stop a man like that; not even a young fellow trying to whip that old T B. A young husband who steps jauntily along to meet success or failure, and who, as he goes, plinks impishly:

"If you don't want me, mama—you sure don't have to stall—'cause I can get more women—than a passenger train can haul—."

CHAPTER SEVENTEEN

"I'm not singin' the blues—

"I'm telling you the hard luck I've had—

"'Cause blues ain't nothin'—

"But a good man feelin' bad—."

So—the officials of a big talking-machine company just happened to tune in on the new North Carolina station at Asheville, WWNC, and were amazed. They knew they'd found a "natural." They hurried to learn the identity of this unknown hillbilly, this sweet singer crooning old-fashioned melodies, and giving gleefully those rowdily humorous ditties, and mournfully those amazing blues that trailed off into sobbing yodels. And they sent a man post haste to sign him up, get his name on the dotted line before some other company could grab him, and then set about at once making a star of him.

Yes?

Well, that's the fantastic tale some imaginative writer spun a few months after all this was supposed to have happened. Other writers, for newspapers and magazines continued to spin it; and the story spread and was believed.

Even Jimmie Rodgers, the first time he heard it, must have considered it interesting. Perhaps the reason why he never contradicted it was that he hated to spoil such a beautiful fable by getting it all messed up with truth.

No miracle, no magic, no Lady Luck set Jimmie Rodgers' eager, restless feet on the path to fame and wealth. Lady Luck gave scant aid. The magic was of his own making. The only miracle was the truly sensational speed with which Destiny lifted him high—once he'd forced her hand. That indeed was unexpected, and so overwhelming that it was some time before we could believe it possible, or even catch our breaths.

But, after that first broadcast there was an almost unbearable period of waiting—for what? Just anything. It seemed to me the whole world had just stopped. We seemed suspended; up in the air. When we came down, where would we land?

My "good luck, darling" had brought him no sudden winnings, either large or small, so far as I could see. Nothing happened. Just nothing.

Naturally, we hadn't expected the city to do a headstand in glee, but it was disconcerting, sort of, to discover that nobody seemed in the least concerned, one way or the other, about my Jimmie being on the air—a real-for-sure radio artist! Had he made good in a big way? Or had he done a complete flop?

He had done—neither one. Yet he did manage to sell the act to go on the air. Not daily, as he had expected, but three times a week, at a salary so small that by the time it was split among the entertainers there was little left for our own family.

To tell the truth, however, I seemed to be the only member of even our family to be greatly disturbed by all this lack of excitement on the part of the radio world.

Jimmie grinned at me: "Aw, kid, you mustn't be lookin' for the whole world to go into a tailspin or go rocketin' to the moon just because your husband is broadcastin'. I'm not worried. I'll make good. Only you have to plow ahead slow and sure sometimes. Get there faster in the end. Why, I think I'm doing pretty fine to have this much of a chance right now. If you could see the old-timers, experienced professionals, just beggin' for a spot. All the time, too, I'm keepin' my eyes open, learning the ropes."

Just the same, he couldn't hide from me the fact that his gaiety was just a little bit forced these days. He was confident he had the goods and would, some day, be able to sell them for a sum sufficient to give his little family security, at least. But he couldn't help being impatient for a look-see at that desired and very necessary security.

His smile was just as wistfully sweet as ever, but a little more sad. His tall frame was getting so thin. His once-smooth, bronzed cheeks were becoming hollowed and alarmingly pale. His once-firm brown hands, with their long sensitive fingers, were now so white and, it seemed to me, nothing but skin and bone. As his lungs weakened, his shoulders seemed to contract. His brown eyes grew larger, more luminous, more beautiful—but frightening to one who loved him so.

I came now to realize the awful import of those two simple words: Wasting away. Wasting—away—and I asked myself frantically: How long? A month? Two? A year?

He tired more easily these days. Resist as he would, there would be times when he had no breath; when fever gripped him so that he had no strength, even to speak to me, and a deep flush burned angrily high on his cheeks.

He worried not a little because he couldn't seem to communicate to his boys his wish for "feeling" their music; couldn't seem to get them to put their hearts into it. But they had not his Irish gift for whimsical gaiety, his Irish soul with its instant response to any emotion. And they had not, could not have, the sufferings, past and present, to leave their searing marks.

Writers were to rave about the heart-throbs in Jimmie Rodgers' throat, and I, alone perhaps, knew all too well what had put them there.

Had he given up all thought of railroading? I think not. It had been a vital part of him for too long. He still hoped, I am sure, that the marvelous day would come when he would be well, strong and whole again, so that once more he could swing joyously to the iron ladder of a swaying box car, his brakeman's lantern twinkling gleefully. I know that from this time on—as well as before—whenever he had the time or strength he sought the haunts of railroad men—as a tired wanderer turns homeward.

MY HUSBAND, JIMMIE RODGERS

Later, on his personal appearance tours, the first eager word he gave out in each town and city was a hearty welcome to railroad men to visit him in his dressing room or at his hotel. If any of them considered this as a big favor to them or as a publicity stunt, they were wrong on both counts. When they came, as many of them did, it was Jimmie Rodgers who was humbly grateful for the favor they did him. They couldn't know his nostalgic longing to hear again the lingo of the silver rails; and how "old Bill" was getting along, and if Tom had gone back to the M & O.

About the third week in June, there in Asheville, in 1927, my Jimmie came home one day without his usual teasingly gay greeting. With a faint smile, a brief kiss, a tired "Hello, Mother," he stretched his long, frail body on the bed and closed his eyes wearily.

Was a congestive chill coming on? I laid my palm on his forehead, on his cheeks. Some temperature, but not alarming. I felt his pulse. Not strong, but not terrifying. But something was wrong—something on his mind. Strangely, he did not, as was his custom, straighten out whatever it was while singing softly and plinking banjo or guitar.

Granting him the privilege of privacy seemed the best way I could help him just then, but I wouldn't leave the house. He might need me. I withdrew, matter-of-factly, to the kitchen and moved around doing little unnecessary things, making no effort to tiptoe or to be too quiet.

Presently Jimmie called me, his voice tired—but determined. "Carrie, if you're not too busy, I wish you'd help me."

When I went in he was sitting on the edge of the bed smoking a cigarette. Not looking at me he said: "Got some writing paper and a couple stamps?"

He would tell me when he could find words. I arranged the writing paper on the little center table, saying: "Shall I write your letters for you?" Often he wished me to, but not this time.

MY HUSBAND, JIMMIE RODGERS

"No—I reckon I'd better write 'em myself—but you can help me figure out what to say." He had a slip of paper in his hands. "I stopped at the music store and got the addresses of the two biggest phonograph companies: Victor and Brunswick. Letters won't do much good, but it's worth a try, maybe. I wish it was so I could get there to 'em and make 'em let me show what I can do." And he added: "I will, too—some of these days, soon."

I was quite sure now what was so distressing my boy, but I said nothing—just listened as if I didn't suspect anything wrong.

"You see, Mother—I've been—let out—up at WWNC. They gave my spot to another entertainer."

"But darling—you made good, didn't you?"

Jimmie said, a little bitterly: "O, I reckon I made good, okay." From his hip pocket he drew a bundle of letters, fan letters, and threw them on the bed. I stared at them as Jimmie added: "Yeah, I made good—kinda—according to those letters. Just same, I've been let out."

Fan letters! A lot of them! More, he admitted, than anybody else on the program had received. So—he had made good! Yet—they'd let him go. Then I remembered what he'd told me about the professionals and the clever amateurs begging for chances. And, as he said, bosses were bosses; they could hire and fire whom they would. They were the ones who must be pleased it seemed.

Well—here were the fan letters—bless them, proving that my Jimmie had pleased the tuners-in, anyway. They hadn't turned the dial, cutting him off. They hadn't laughed at him; they'd laughed with him—and sobbed with him.

Before the letters were ready to post he was called to the telephone. He said: "Come with me, Mother. I'm—just kind of tired, I guess."

At the phone, my arms around him, protecting him from I didn't know what, I saw his tired face break into a pleased smile.

"Well, thanks, old man! I'd sure like to. Only trouble is—." In spite of himself then, in his bitter disappointment, his voice broke a little. "Fact is, I'm sorry, but I can't. I'm always glad to oblige with request numbers—but you see—they've let me out up there. Put some one else in my spot."

The voice at the other end of the wire was protesting—in a way that pleased my boy. He said: "Well, I sure thank you, anyway. But I'll be on the air again—some time. Watch for me."

It was a writer, Jimmie told me, a columnist, asking him to repeat one of his lullabies, saying how much he and his wife enjoyed it.

"Gee, Honey," I exclaimed. "If he'd just phoned like that—before they let you go!"

To that Jimmie grinned. "Shucks, Sweetheart—it doesn't matter. I'll get on some place else. Lots of other stations—other places. Like I told you; I've learned a heap. Easier now to book dates around. If I can't get 'em in town we'll go to the woods. Keep goin'. That's the only way. Anyway, just think! I can bill the hillbilly ork now as—popular radio artists. That's worth something."

CHAPTER EIGHTTEEN

"I've been from several places—

"And I'm goin' to be from here—."

"Well, Mother—as the farmer said: Reckon we've dug jist 'bout all the taters in this row."

"That means—throw my things together?"

"Right, first guess, kid."

So—we consoled each other for having to leave Asheville by pretending to be gay about it. But I knew, even if he didn't tell me, how disappointed, how near heartbreak he really was. But of course he had not the least idea of giving up. It must have been one of Jimmie's Irish ancestors who, while lying on his back, with both eyes swollen closed and an antagonist sitting on his chest, pounding him heartily, yelled: "Give up, is it? Sure, why should I give up when 'tis meself has ye licked so bad I can't see ye at all, at all."

But—it is disconcerting to know you've taken one step forward only to discover that you've been shoved, without warning, ten steps backward. To Jimmie Rodgers it appeared to mean a retracing of lost ground; and time was so precious, just then, to a sick man determined to provide for his family.

If Spring is not far behind Winter, at least Winter comes first; and although it was just turning July—Winter loomed before us, starkly. Always before there had been the chance of a few weeks, or months perhaps, with the railroads. We both knew that was out of the question now.

Daily I felt that my brief business course was slipping away from me; although I tried to keep my stenographic ability in good working order, busy as I was with washing, ironing, mending, and cooking three meals—sometimes four—a day for three people and often more. And I wondered if I'd ever make real use of my shorthand. Would Jimmie's yodels ever be able to keep us from starving? Would they, could they, provide shelter and clothing? And—what about our little daughter's education?

Well—we ewere "taking to the road." Wherever night caught us, that would be our home—for the remainder of our lives, it seemed. Mother had begged us to let her keep Nita during the school term, at least. But Jimmie told me wistfully: "Let's keep Baybo with us as long as we can, anyway. If we're not set, time school starts— well, of course, we've got to do what's best for her—even if we have to be without our baby for a few months. But—by next year—."

By next year—what? My heart was torn with conflicting emotions; bitterness, resentment; both curiously mingled with pity—and with pride. And I wrote my mother: "Don't be surprised if we let you have your wish." And I made up my mind to do my best to get the little family, now "taking to the road," headed west by south, but mostly south—back to Meridian.

It saddened us both, in more ways than one, to know we had to leave Asheville. We'd made pleasant friendships among some of the young married folks, as we did wherever we went, penniless vagabonds though we were, most of the time. And Jimmie had good friends and pals, Fred Jones and others in the police department. Jimmie's brother, Talmadge, is with the police department in Meridian, so he always felt "closely related" to all policemen. Too, there were his cronies among the railroad men.

Jimmie helped me all he could—by getting in my way every minute while I was obeying orders, trying to get packed; and I stewed about it affectionately, loving him just for being there.

As he closed his guitar case and fastened it, he said: "Funny I don't hear from either one of those talking machine folks. Kind of wish I could know before we leave. Might change our plans. I'll run up to WWNC and get what mail's up there for me—if any."

If any! Just another sizable bunch was all. Letters, fan letters, still coming in. Raves about his sobbing yodeling, about the sweetness of his crooning lullabies; and waves of raves about—of all things—"T for Texas." Yes, Jimmie Rodgers had impudently confided to the ether public his troubles with Thelma; had told them he was goin' to shoot poor Thelma, just to see her jump and fall! Had told 'em—and made 'em like it. They asked for more. And more. And why didn't he come back on the air? Where was he? Where was he going?

Well—to the last not even we ourselves knew the answer. For there, at last, were the replies from Brunswick and from Victor, thanking him for remembering them, but politely uninterested; they had all the talent they needed.

Jimmie read those letters to me while I was whisking the last few things together. Then he said, smiling a bit ruefully: "Well, Mr. Brunswick and Mr. Victor, maybe I'll get a chance to meet you some day—and show you what big hands I got." Then he grinned and fanned his praise letters across the bed, saying: "Sugar, when'll we ever get time now to answer all these?"

"But—you must, Jimmie!"

"Sure thing! Gosh—it's swell of 'em, and I sure appreciate their letters. They're the only kind of hands we 'popular radio stars' can ever know about. Takes time and trouble—and stamps too.—Say, I've been kind of thinkin' maybe it'd be a good thing to head for Baltimore and try the stations there."

Baltimore! And in my own mind, we'd already headed west by south; mostly south.

MY HUSBAND, JIMMIE RODGERS

Before he'd been replaced at WWNC Jimmie had written to some of the folks back home, boasting boyishly: "Told you I'd amount to something some day." And having been dismissed so soon after, her may have felt a bit uncomfortable about meeting Meridian folks face to face; at least, until they'd had time to forget that letter.

Still, all those fan letters were most consoling. They convinced him anew that he was right. This was his alley and no one should head him out of it. He'd make that boast good yet.

Now, he was taking his hillbilly ork to the woods. We might wind up in Baltimore or Key West. Or we might just keep on going forever and ever—and ever—.

We had no car of our own, of course. Had never owned one since that first little second-hand Dodge, over which I'd cried in secret when we had to let it go "to live on." I knew positively that my poor sick boy could never buy me that proud new Buick he'd once promised me—blue or any color. Every year the new models seemed prettier and prettier, and every year we both turned to look after them as they flashed by, our eyes more and more wistful. But Jimmie hadn't forgotten his promise. "You wait, Sugar. I said I'd buy you one some day; and I will, too—some day."

So now into the big old sedan belonging to one of the musicians working with Jimmie we piled ourselves, our child, our luggage and Jimmie's collection of stringed instruments. The old sedan gobbled us in somehow, in spite of the fact it contained, already, the other three boys, their luggage and instrument cases. My feet had to rest, most uncomfortably, on Jimmie's old guitar—and how could I, or any of us, suspect how soon it was to win fame and affection all its own?

As we headed out of town Jimmie turned to look back. He favored the clouds above Asheville with a humorous salute, then sang mournfully:

"Will they have respect for a hobo—in the land that lies hidden up there?"

CHAPTER NINETEEN

"I'm going to pack my grip—
"And head to that way—
"You'll see me hangin' 'round—some day—."

When Jimmie Rodgers had flung back his cavalier salute of farewell to Asheville and had crooned his mournful bit of song, he added: "Gosh, I sure hate to leave that town. Swell folks there."

Asheville had been neither glad nor sad to see us go, but why should it be either, anyway? How could Asheville suspect that "genius had strolled among them"? Particularly, when not even the genius, himself, suspected it? Well, Jimmie knew he was no genius, then or ever. All he knew was that he he had done his best to make good with what humble gifts he possessed; although he was confident that he had "just sort of happened" on an unusual method of expressing the music that was in his Irish heart, and he was shrewd enough to gage its potential value. If enough folks could hear him, and would approve, as he was convinced they would, it would mean for himself and "his two" that longed-for and very necessary security; rest, freedom from petty, irritating worries. In Asheville, at WWNC, he had been so sure he all but had it. But—he'd been wrong.

So—we drove away; the young tubercular ex-brakeman and his wife and child, with the three young musicians who, with Jimmie Rodgers, made up the humble hillbilly ork, The Jimmie Rodgers Entertainers.

On the road. Wildcatting. Barnstorming. Playing the sticks, the tanks, the jerkwaters, the turkeys. These, I learned, were the professional showman's terms when small "amusement enterprises," such as The Jimmie Rodgers Entertainers, moved about from small town to village to crossroads, stopping to "show" wherever they could; wherever and for whatever they could get.

Humble itinerant musicians though they were, Jimmie included, they spoke now always in terms of "the profession." (To a showman there is only one profession!) They observed, too, with much care, the time-honored traditions of the show world; especially its superstitions. Often I just didn't know what it was all about! But I was beginning to get my first glimpses behind the scenes of that most fascinating world, a world I was to know quite well indeed, in the very near future.

Once, moved to song, I began humming gaily, "Home, Sweet Home"—but such wails and howls instantly assailed my ears that I was not only mystified, but fairly horrified; until it was explained to me that it meant we'd all be going home! I didn't say so, but I couldn't help thinking that would be no great calamity.

When I asked: "Why? You boys play it every night, nearly—at the end of a dance; all orchestras do!" They assured me: "That's different. It's okay to use it as a dance-tag number, a chaser. But—no other time."

Several times I heard one or another of them yelp vigorously at some poor unsuspecting kid, who hovered near, wistfully watching and idly playing a mouth harp. That, it seemed, would "queer the house, sure."

And once I heard a yowl: "Who threw whose hat on the bed? Betcha we don't make the nut tonight!" If we didn't get the nut—the overhead—didn't make expenses, I knew quite well that Jimmie Rodgers' "two" would be left "in soak"—left in town with all the personal luggage as security for hotel bills, while the breadwinners hustled on to some other "spot" to try to collect enough to "life us out." And if they didn't get enough?—Ever?

But we were young, life was good, and we could manage, somehow, to see the humorous side of everything—even an old sedan with four flat feet! The mountain air was sweet and cool; crackers and cheese by the roadside can be ambrosia fit for the gods; and hot coffee out of a cheap vacuum bottle, nectar fit for goddesses.

I had been so sure this sort of life on the road, through the mountains in summertime, would be good medicine for an eager, ambitious young husband, with wasting-away body and sick lungs; but Jimmie had now so little time to give that body needed rest and no chance at all, it seemed, to rest his mind. He couldn't catch up with his big worries; there were too many small immediate worries to pester him. Securing bookings; consecutive dates. Getting the "tonighters," the heralds, printed, and saving out money to pay for them. Even when he could find a few free moments, he was too exhausted to even reach for his guitar and tease "his two" with phrases from his rowdy songs; too tired to yodel a gay retort or to pull my hair or tweak Nita's ear and "whoo-whoo-oo."

Happy and carefree as he'd always been; now tired and sick, it seemed there were so many annoying little things constantly happening to distress him. Mostly he was patient and cheerful; but I didn't like to see him push his plate of restaurant food away, frowning at it. There was not other food to be had; no delicacies for a sick boy. There was seldom time to wait for a special order, and even if there had been, there was no money.

No matter how carefully he prepared his copy for the printers, they'd make annoying mistakes. Jimmie Rodgers was, all through his professional life, much distressed by the misspelling of his two names and of the word "yodel," with its variations.

On this barnstorming tour, having his very first publicity, cheap though it was, one of the very first printing jobs delivered to him had his first name spelled J-i-m-m-e-y. Others would persist in omitting the "d" from Rodgers. Small matters? Not to a professional artist whose name is his trade mark. And even if Webster does give "yodle" as a secondary spelling, Jimmie preferred and insisted on "yodel"; but in spite of all he could say or do about it, sometimes his manager or his agent, or some one, somewhere, would overlook that, to him, most important little detail. To Jimmie Rodgers "yodler" was "yoddler." As he grinned once, somewhat disgustedly: "Hang the luck! I don't yoddle!"

Just then his yodels weren't putting us on top of the world; nor did it seem likely that they ever would. But at least they were helping to keep us from starving. At every little concert, in wayside school auditoriums, Jimmie's solo numbers stopped the show, even without his yodeling. But—when he gave them his yodels—.

Once, after a performance, Jimmie said to me: "Mother, I don't know if they were kidding me or not; but kind of sounded to me like they ovationed me!"

They weren't kidding. I sat among them and heard their eager comments, saw the delight in their eyes, the pleased smiles on their lips. I heard one girl at a mountain resort tell her escort: "Boy, can that fella yodel! I'll say! Listen to the blues when he sobs those yodels!"

Her companion said: "That's a new way to spill your blues. Yodel 'em! That blue yodeler's there!"

Blue yodeler! Of course! Why hadn't we thought of that before? That would be a keen way to bill himself, I thought.

But Jimmie was so loyal to his boys; his hillbilly ork. He was pleased that his solo efforts were so well accepted; but he refused to give himself individual publicity. So, on all billing matter, consisting solely of those minute hand-bills which showmen term "tonighters," printed on slips of red, blue, green, yellow, pink and lavender paper, appeared simply the professional title of the little band of musicians; The Jimmie Rodgers Entertainers.

Blue yodels. That's what they were; those heartbreaking yodels he'd first flung out over the Texas plains, testing his lung against the Texas winds as we drove gaily westward in our decrepit little Dodge; westward to Arizona, to Tucson. Blue yodels.

We'd both decided then that they were "pretty good." Now other folks, lots of folks were liking them, too. And they liked also that amazingly natural mellow train whistle he'd perfected on that very same trip.

The going, that July of 1927, was, as the boys said, "plenty tough." If they could have worked every night we would all have gotten by, very nicely. But it seemed impossible to arrange bookings for more than two or three consecutive nights. Yet, when we "laid off," of course our expenses went on just the same.

Therefore, the inevitable day came when Mrs. Jimmie Rodgers and little Miss Carrie Anita Rodgers were left "on the lot," and with the luggage, while the bread-winners hurried on, not knowing when they could return with sufficient cash to get us "out of soak." Tomorrow, of course—sure—if possible. If—.

Idling around in the little general store I lingered in the radio and phonograph department, since my husband, Jimmie Rodgers, was now a popular radio artist. At least, so the tonighters stated—and as those bundles of fan letters seemed to prove. And there I had my first thrill of being recognized by a "towner" as a trouper.

The man said: "O—you're one of the radio entertainers that showed here last night, aren't you? I wanted to go—but our baby was sick."

I told him: "Well, I'm with them, but not one of the artists. My husband, Jimmie Rodgers, is."

The man showed eager interest. "Is that so? I heard him over WWNC a while back. He's sure good. Folks keep asking me for his phonograph records, but they don't seem to be listed in any catalog I have. Maybe he's with some group, though—like the Southern Fiddlers, or something. What company's he with?"

I said, as calmly as I could: "Well, he's had some correspondence with the Brunswick folks and with the Victor people, but he hasn't decided yet. He's waiting until we get up near New York."

Then the man told me: "One of our local singers was telling me a while ago that a talent scout for Victor is bringing portable equipment down to Bristol and will give auditions. I wonder if your husband knows? It might save him a trip to New York—unless he's going there, anyway."

Did that blessed man suspect the truth? I believe he did.

But—where in the world was Jimmie Rodgers? I was frantic to spill the grand news. Where—where—was he? And where was Bristol? As far as I was concerned, it wouldn't be on the map officially until the Victor talent scout was actually there and my Jimmie was actually provoking to him what The Jimmie Rodgers Entertainers could do.

As far as I could learn from the road map, Bristol was in Virginia—or Tennessee— or perhaps both. You could take your choice, it seemed.

I just couldn't sleep. Until after three in the morning I wrote letters, mended, embroidered, did everything, trying to still my frantic wish to get the news to my boy.

And—in he came! Not looking tired at all, nor even worried; but happy and confident.

In a rush I began: "Jimmie, there's a—."

My young husband laughed softly, put his hand over my mouth, and chuckled.

"Throw your things together, kid. Soon's it's daylight, we're leaving here for—Bristol."

CHAPTER TWENTY

"Once I had a sweetheart—

"A sweetheart brave and true—."

We couldn't get to Bristol in a couple of hours, as I wished; nor in a couple of days. For a time it seemed that we were unlikely to make it in even a couple of weeks!

We had to barnstorm our way, stopping wherever the boys could get a chance to earn enough for beds, gas, oil and such food as we simply had to have; all the time hoping and praying that the old sedan wouldn't go haywire and that we wouldn't have to lay out cash for even used tubes or casings.

But—at long last we did drive into Bristol. Bristol Town, which very magnanimously gives itself to Virginia and Tennesese, half and half, with the State Line serving as its main street, State Street. Bristol—where fortune or misfortune awaited us.

And I wailed: "O dear; I do hope that Victor man is still here! But what would he think if he could see us now! This tired, dirty, crumpled bunch of tin can tourists coming to town, depending for their very dear lives, almost, on just a word from him."

Jimmie grinned: "Shucks, Mother, why should he care one way or the other? If we can show him the goods, that's all he's looking for."

Our smallest daughter, Miss Anita Rodgers, spoke then: "Yes, but Daddy! Maybe he doesn't know who we are."

Jimmie said solemnly: "Nope, don't reckon he does. Just who are we, anyway? Anybody 'round here know?"

MY HUSBAND, JIMMIE RODGERS

"Why, Daddy. We're national broadcasting artists!"

So—tired, dirty, crumpled and laughing, we drove straight to a modest little cafe on State Street to "coffee up." Often you can get all the information you need while coffee-ing up.

Yes, the Victor man was still there. Second floor over that brick, down a block and across the street—on the Tennessee side.

We bustled out, bent on a frantic cleaning up for this most important occasion. But first, rooms! Jimmie Rodgers and family considered themselves lucky, indeed, to find a pleasant room up over a bakery; a front room in Virginia from which we could stare across, above the "traffic" of State Street, to the tall windows of that glamorous "second floor over that brick" in Tennessee, where the talent scout for Victor was making magic for a few lucky unknowns.

It was still early in the day when Jimmie, with his hillbilly ork, all hurriedly pressed, clean-shirted, freshly barbered, went hurrying across from Virginia to Tennessee to learn their fate.

An account in a magazine of national circulation, some time ago, stated that Jimmie Rodgers approached his man sick, unshaven, unkempt. Jimmie was indeed a sick man. But personal neatness and cleanliness were to him, always, among the very essentials of existence. No other condition was to be endured. He had a gift for wearing clothes, even though shabby and threadbare, so that he appeared always well dressed. So on this occasion, while he was threadbare, pershaps, he was otherwise as natty as he could make himself.

When Jimmie came back to me, that day in the beginning of August, in 1927, his step jaunty, his eyes shining, I knew that he had good news.

Yep, the man had consented to give them an audition! And if he approved of the hillbilly ork, The Jimmie Rodgers Entertainers, he would make a test record. And if the Victor folks at the factory in Camden, New Jersey, liked their efforts—well.

MY HUSBAND, JIMMIE RODGERS

And then Jimmie told me: "You'd never guess what the man's name is. Peer!"

"Yes?" Just what of it, I wondered.

"Well, Hon—don't you see? He's working with the Victor people."

"Yes, I know, of course—but—."

"Well, gosh, Mother! Victor—Peer. Sort of looks to me like those two names would be pretty nice for me to be connected with. A victor is a winner, isn't he? And a peer is the top of the heap."

I laughed and teased: "Then maybe you'd better change your name to something like—Jimmie Starr!"

"No sirree! Jimmie Rodgers is my name, no matter what happens. Good enough for me."

"But," I demanded impatiently. "When, Jimmie—when?"

"Huh? O—be ready for us in just a little while. 'Bout an hour, he said."

All the way into Bristol there had been lively argument as to just which numbers in the repertoire of The Jimmie Rodgers Entertainers it would be advisable to offer the Victor man—if he consented to listen to them. Not "T for Texas," of course, as that was one of Jimmie's solo numbers; nor "The Soldier's Sweetheart," nor any of his own compositions.

I was wishing it would be possible for Jimmie to show the man how he could put over a solo; one of his crooning lullabies, or even one of his rowdy novelties. But of course, I knew he couldn't and wouldn't. Because the hillbilly ork was a group, working together; all for one—one for all.

I wondered then, however, just where the boys were. Usually they were right at Jimmie's heels. But—where were they—in an exciting time like this?

Jimmie told me they'd gone down the street "to see a guy they knew." And he added, grinning: "They'll meet me up there, don't worry. They'll be there right on the dot.

MY HUSBAND, JIMMIE RODGERS

So I told him: "Good luck, darling," and he gave his straw hat a still more jaunty tilt and hurried out, his guitar under his arm. But as I heard him hurrying, happily confident, down the stairs just beneath our room I heard also—that pitiful cough. And I prayed: "Please, God—. Please!"

When I hurried to look out the window I couldn't see which way he'd gone. Across the street, at the entrance of that two-story brick, that "magic land," I could see no one I knew. Others, coming and going; but not one familiar figure; not one of the hillbilly ork, neither Jimmie nor any of the other musicians. Perhaps, during that moment I'd closed my eyes, looking to God, the four of them had met and hurried on up, out of my sight.

But then I heard—a pitiful cough—and stumbling feet—coming back up the stairwell!

The door opened slowly. My boy came in, a tired, wistful, heartbreaking little smile on his lips; but none at all in his brown eyes—.

I got to my feet, shaking; but found I had no words to say, nor voice to say them.

Jimmie laid his guitar aside, slumped his long frail body tiredly into a rocker, his back to the window that looked on Tennesee. I saw his fingers trembling as he lighted a cigarette.

Again I prayed to God—to tell me the right thing to say. He must have told me: Say nothing, child.

Suddenly Jimmie got to his feet, flinging his cigarette aside. He told me, his words tumbling over themselves.

"The boys have made arrangements with Mr. Peer to make a test record—without me!"

For a moment he looked at me like a hurt little boy, puzzled over why somebody should have injured him unexpectedly, then continued:

"I guess I don't blame them. If they go over—if they click—they'll get more.

MY HUSBAND, JIMMIE RODGERS

Dividing by three is more per each than dividing by four. And it's like they told me. They worked as a trio before they met we, so they're used to it. They know just what they have to offer. They've already had an audition, so it's all set for them. They're to record in the morning."

My thoughts were wild. How could they? O—how could they treat him so? I wanted to protest, to hold him close in my arms, to speak my sympathy, assure him of my love and loyalty. But—he knew those things; and I saw that, just then, he didn't need them!

Jimmie Rodgers was taking his uppercut, his sock on the chin, gamely, as always. He was busy—fighting through; puzzling out the next move; how to tear down that block others had raised in his alley.

After all, though, it seemed simple—or was it? Anyway, my Jimmie suddenly clenched his fists, drew a big breath, and told me: "Mother, I'm going over and camp on Mr. Peer's trail—until I make him give me a chance to show him what I can do—alone! Look for me—when you see me coming. And, Mother—wish me good luck again, for God's sake!"

The pleading, the earnest prayer in my young husband's voice was heart-breaking, but I told him again, smiling, in words husky with tears: "Good luck, darling!" And as I heard his determined steps going down the stairs, I added: "And God bless you, my beloved."

And some way I just knew Mr. Peer would listen; would give my boy—his chance!

And I thought: "Oh, I do hope Jimmie will play and sing 'T for Texas,' if Mr. Peer will listen."

Suddenly I went scrambling through our luggage for all those blessed fan letters! If only Jimmie had taken those with him! Then Mr. Peer would see!

I didn't know just what to do. Should I "take my nerve with me" and venture over there to that "magic land" with my Jimmie's fan letters from his pitifully few broadcasting appearances over WWNC? If I did, what would Mr. Peer think? And maybe I'd make an entrance on the wrong cue—and queer my Jimmie's chances!

Undecided, yet filled with frantic longing to help, I glued my nose to our window in Virginia and my eyes to those magic windows over in Tennessee. And could see nothing.

But I heard—once again—determined footsteps on the stairs—coming back up. The door opened and Jimmie stepped inside, a curious light in his brown eyes; an almost mischievous little quirk trembling on his lips.

I have a few superstitions of my own. Now, with a small chill, I gasped: "Darling— if you forgot something—sit down quick—and count ten!"

Surprised, Jimmie protested: "Aw, shucks, Mother!" But he sat down obediently. Got up again and hurried to the door his hand on the knob—and, stood there, chuckling. He told me: "I didn't forget anything, though. I came back to tell you I remembered something! Or maybe—just for a minute—we both forgot something. Forgot to remember—to take it with a grin!"

The fan letters! Laughing, I poked a bundle of them into his coat pocket. And I was alone. But added to the muffled sound of those eager, receding footfalls, I heard a subdued plinking and a softly caroled:

"He said goodbye, little darling—to France I must go—."

CHAPTER TWENTY-ONE

"Will the hobo ride with the rich man—

"Will he always have money to spare—?"

A simple matter to heave that block aside? Not if you view it in the right per-spective. R. S. Peer was—and is—a business man. A busy man could scarcely be expected to listen to the troubles and yearnings of every Tom-Dick-and-Harry who swarmed through that temporary studio in Bristol that first week in August, 1927, each individual convinced that all he or she needed to become famous and wealthy was to persuade or trick "the Victor man" into lending them his ear.

Moreover, it was, of course, absolutely necessary for Mr. Peer to adhere strictly to the number of test records he had set as his limit for submission to the factory at Camden. The Victor officials had faith in his good judgment; but nevertheless, each and every record he submitted to them was his gamble. If they turned it down he was out both time and expense. When he picked a loser, that was his hard luck; but when he did discover a winner, all concerned, including the artist, were to the good.

The deciding board at the factory did not always see eye to eye with Mr. Peer—nor hear ear to ear with him. They were bound by no contract to pass favorably on all tests he submitted. And even those they okayed did not always click with the public.

After all, it was the men and women who shelled out their six bits each for those black discs—throughout this land and foreign countries—who could, and some-times did, decide thumbs down on a solo artist or a group of artists.

Thus, artists desiring fame and fortune, or even something like security, had to please not only Mr. Peer, but also "Mr. Victor," and then, having done both, could be knocked into a cocked hat by Mr. and Mrs. Public.

That day, when Jimmie left me, intent on camping on Mr. Peer's trail until he could make him listen, I reminded myself that a conservative business man is not likely to be overpleased, having made a business agreement with a group of four, and later consented to deal with only three of them, if still later—the fourth member of the group comes trailing back, whining his troubles. He is, I thought, more likely to throw the whole matter out of the window and forget it.

One thing was certain. The Jimmie Rodgers Entertainers, as an organization, was definitely in the discard. Jimmie had not put it there, but even though I sensed how this scrapping of his beloved little hillbilly ork had hurt him, still I was glad. Jimmie Rodgers was now, once again, completely on his own. I knew well enough the difficulties he would have to overcome to "make Mr. Peer listen"—but I had supreme faith in his succeeding, eventually. He had to! He would. That bulldog tenacity of his, combined with that wistful charm, would win for him—where others might fail.

And suddenly, my nose pressed against the screen of our window in Virginia, my eyes glued to those mysterious windows in Tennessee, I thought: "O, if I could just have given my poor sick boy a son! A son, soon to grow into manhood, to stand by his father, to think for him, to give him man-person companionship. Some one to depend on. Some one sturdy and strong and determined—instead of "his two"—a weak, shy woman and a small girl-child.

I visualized, then, our beloved and idolized Carrie Anita, with her hair of gold and eyes of deep blue, and her vigorous, lithe little body. And I thought; even prayed: "Give her time. She'll be a son-daughter for my Jimmie!"

Staring intently at those inscrutable windows in Tennessee, visualizing the man-child, stalwart and strong, I so wished I could have given my husband, quite suddenly I caught my breath. Was it my imagination—that apparition over there in one of those windows? It might have been Jimmie Rodgers' own son, that tall, little body, the face too white, but so youthful of line, the lips wide over white teeth in an unmistakably boyish grin.

He was making, for my benefit, curious motions, guarded—but insistent.

A match! He wanted a match for his cigarette!

Not bothering my head with silly questions as to why he could not borrow a match or a light from somebody over there in that fascinating place, I snatched a penny box of matches from the dresser, opened the door—and ran smack-dab into our greatly excited girl-child, clinging to the hand of an equally excited visitor— Lottie Mae Rodgers!

Without even so much as a "Howdy," I gasped: "Jimmie! He's over there! He wants a match!"

Lottie Mae, who had come hundreds of miles to see us, had long ago ceased to expect anything approaching sanity where we were concerned. She merely said instantly: "Let's go."

Together, then, the three of us went scurrying breathlessly from Virginia to Tennessee, to carry Jimmie Rodgers the momentous gift of a match.

Lottie Mae, now Mrs. Lawrence C. Mixon, of York, Alabama, was Jimmie's half sister, but Jimmie and I, both, always spoke and thought of her as our sister. Jimmie's father had gotten his daughter a pass to visit us in Asheville, but I'd had to send her word about our leaving, and when I knew about Bristol I sent her further word, telling of our hopes. And here she was—to help if she could. Kindly, sympathetic, sensible, as always.

After all, though, there was little for us to see—up there in that mysterious place. Nothing particularly exciting, or out of the ordinary, I mean. A well-dressed, pleasant-faced man was sitting by a desk, speaking into a telephone. Somewhere behind him—and what really astonished us—was our Jimmie, impudently greeting us by waving a lighted cigarette.

He leaned forward then and whispered to me: "I just wanted you to be here to watch me make my first record."

His first record! It might easily be his first, last—and only. But at least, it would be his first! He knew, whether or not he ever made another, this moment of watching him make his first would be, for me—for us all—a pleasurable thrill which could never be duplicated. Thoughtful Jimmie always remembered to include me in the little excitements and adventures that played so important a part in our lives.

Just being there was, for me, one of the big moments of my life—even though watching him make his first record, was, in itself, no more than looking at him while he confidently strummed his guitar and sang into a little microphone. It was a grand moment for Lottie Mae, too; and something for our daughter, young as she was, to remember.

But—Jimmie had already given to that little "mike" his first number—before we could get up there. So, our first real thrill was hearing the "play-back."

And through that very same little "mike," which appeared, to our unsophisticated eyes, so incapable of anything, came Jimmie's voice! So clear and sweet; every word so distinct! There beside me sat my boy—smiling. And why shouldn't he be smiling with satisfaction—when every one of us, Mr. Peer included, realized that, without doubt, Jimmie Rodgers had a perfect recording voice?

Still—I found myself not a little dismayed. It was seldom that I ever criticized or questioned my husband's judgment, but this occasion was I felt, of extra importance. So, when I realized he had used for the first of his two numbers—and with only two allowed him—that thousand-years-old lullaby "Sleep, Baby, Sleep," I was decidedly uneasy.

Surely, though, for his second number he would use something—well something bright and lively, or something quaintly humorous, like "Way Out on the Mountain" perhaps, or even "T for Texas." But—would he dare confide to that august deciding board at the Victor factory the details of his troubles with poor Thelma?

Anyway, the listeners-in had liked it—over WWNC.

Before I could make up my mind what to say or do about it, or ask Lottie Mae what she thought about it, I heard Mr. Peer saying to Jimmie: "Haven't you any of your own compositions you can use? You'll get extra royalties, you know."

I settled back at ease. Now, I thought, Jimmie will give his mournfully rowdy "T for Texas."

But—he was plinking his guitar softly and singing; and I was glad he could not see the consternation in my eyes nor hear the little choked gasp in my throat.

Standing there before that microphone, one foot on a chair, his eyes closed, Jimmie Rodgers was singing as if he'd forgotten everything and everybody in the world—except a boy who'd gone to "that awful German war"—and a girl sobbing in heartbroken agony: "My darling dear was dead—."

CHAPTER TWENTY-TWO

"I like Mississippi—

"I'm a fool about Tennessee—."

I must have been in some sort of a daze; because, before I realized it, Jimmie had finished and was talking quietly with Mr. Peer.

My ears were still hearing his song, but I was remembering also a childhood phrase; a rueful or taunting saying used when it was too late to correct an error: "The train's gone."

Here was Jimmie Rodgers staking his future, perhaps, and our future as well—Nita's and mine—on an old timey lullaby and an out-of-date war ballad, pathetic in its very simplicity. These—when he had a daring novelty like "T for Texas," with its blue yodels those city people at the mountain resort had so raved about. "T for Texas"—that had so delighted, because of its very audacity, all those listeners-in over WWNC.

I found my breath; stirred myself to action, and deliberately dug into my husband's pocket for the selected few, out of all those wonderful letters, which I had given him such a little while ago to help him sell himself.

With these in my hands I said to Mr. Peer: "O, please—please let him make another record. He didn't give you "T for Texas"—and that's the one everybody's so crazy about. It shows what he can really do! Those two he's given you—why, almost anybody could do those. Please let him make one more."

Mr. Peer was interested, kindly—but very, very firm. "I never make more than

MY HUSBAND, JIMMIE RODGERS

one test record for anybody. That's an ironclad rule. Sorry."

Maddingly—Jimmie just smiled—a small, pleasant smile.

Woman-like, I persisted: "But, Mr. Peer. Just everything in the world depends on this! You don't know! Give him a chance to show how he can yodel the blues. He's different!"

Mr. Peer said patiently: "If this first one clicks he can do his blue yodel number for his second recording. Sorry—but that's all I can do, Mrs. Rodgers."

The train had gone! How could there be any possibility for his second recording if there wasn't even a fair chance for his first to get over?

Jimmie was, just then, trying to control a little spasm of coughing. I saw Mr. Peer glance at him—pityingly. Lottie Mae gripped my hand. And I wished I could rid myself of that sobbing phrase: "My darling dear was—dead—."

But I had been permitted to watch my husband make his first record. And I could see how happy he was; supremely content. So I put aside my worries. And I put aside my chills of foreboding. The thing to do now was congratulate him with happy smiles; assure him of my stout belief in his ultimate success.

Something whispered to me: "You ought to be ashamed of yourself! Even this much of a chance doesn't come every day to an ex-brakeman with sick lungs. Be glad! Don't just act glad: Be glad!"

So—I was; honestly glad, thankful that, at least for the moment, my boy was happily content, secure in his belief that at long last his eager feet were firmly planted in his own private alley.

Then came something which astounded me; something which even yet I must confess I don't quite understand. I was too happy over it all, too excited, to ask questions, then or later. But—I saw that Mr. Peer was explaining a paper to my husband and offering it to him for his signature. A contract!

I saw that Jimmie was quite as surprised as I was! Then, after Jimmie had put his name to the dotted line, Mr. Peer was, I realized, doing another amazing thing.

MY HUSBAND, JIMMIE RODGERS

Opening his billfold, he selected a gold-colored piece of currency and put it into Jimmie's hand. And Jimmie was saying: "Gosh, that's fine! Thanks, Mr. Peer. We sure need that twenty right now."

Twenty dollars! I had almost forgotten there was so much money in the world—all in one place.

Was that Mr. Peer's customary procedure when, as a talent scout, he'd approved of some unknown musician and had decided to make a test record for submission to the Victor factory? Or was it that, on this occasion, satisfied that he'd made a "find," he was willing to take more than his usual gamble? I don't know. All I know is that he gave Jimmie Rodgers a much-needed and appreciated twenty-dollar bill.

He gave him, also, a contract which, although it was really nothing more than a sort of short-time option on his services, subjecting him to a call for a second re-cording—if it ever came—was still a "contract."

As we were leaving, Mr. Peer suggested that it would be wise for use to locate somewhere within easy reach of Camden. When Jimmie received his "call," he told us, all expenses would be met by the Victor Company, including transportation and hotel bills.

And it was a big relief to know that!

Through it all our small daughter had been unusually quiet, taking it all in, in wide-eyed interest, asking no questions—for once—but, we knew, storing them up by the dozen for future airing. She was not frightened by the strange surround-ings. Not our little Carrie Anita! Poor child, she'd never known anything much but strange surroundings.

However, just at the last, she did ask a question; just one. As Jimmie reached for his old guitar—which had that day, unsuspected by any of us, already started on its own path to fame—Nita sidled close to her father and loud-whispered: "Daddy, when are you going to phonograph?"

MY HUSBAND, JIMMIE RODGERS

Jimmie gave his guitar into my keeping, took his child up in his arms, and loud-whispered back to her, solemnly: "Daughter, your honorable father, Jimmie Rodgers, has already phonographed."

To which she wailed: "Daddy! I wanted to see you!"

Grinning, he whispered: "Hush, darling. Your parent is now a Victor recording artist."

As we hurried, an excited, elated group, back across State Street to our room in Virginia, Jimmie said: "Gosh! I sort of hate to leave Tennessee."

Then he added: "Nothin' more there for me, I guess. It's all in Camden now."

We had so suddenly become personages of such vast importance—to ourselves—that it seemed strange nobody on State Street was paying the slightest bit of attention to us! It didn't seem possible that such an upheaval could occur in the lives of two struggling, puzzled human beings—and the world go right on about its business unheeding—and uncaring.

Back in Virginia, Lottie Mae had something to say to us.

"Listen, children. I'm going to take Nita home with me for a little visit and we are going tonight. You kids must locate somewhere near Camden, and you will need time to get set and get on your feet again. It'll be quite a while, you know, before you can expect any hard cash in hand from your records, Jimmie. Mother Rodgers and I will enjoy having her and I know Nita wants to see her Grandpa! If you like, we can start her in school there in Geiger, or we can take her to your mother, Carrie, and she can go to school there in Meridian. Then, when you get set and want her, we'll all see that she gets to you, wherever you are, all safe and sound and sweet as ever."

Well—I had, in Asheville, made secret plans along that line; yet now, right along with Jimmie, I found myself rebelling. Of course, we deeply appreciated the kindness and thoughtfulness which had prompted the offer—yet—it seemed we just couldn't bear to let our baby go away from us.

MY HUSBAND, JIMMIE RODGERS

Jimmie looked at me pitifully and said: "Mother!"

But—quite suddenly I could see into the future. Not far; just a little way. Lottie Mae was right. We'd need time to get set; to get on our feet again. Where we were going to be, or for how long in one place, or what we were going to use for money to buy food and shelter through the coming winter, time alone could tell. If the deciding board—if the old-time lullaby and "Soldier's Sweetheart"—if—if—IF—.

All we could have, even if his record went on the market and clicked, for several months perhaps would be whatever dates Jimmie could manage to book as a single entertainer. But—where? Who'd want a sick boy with a bad cough? A threadbare, gaunt-cheeked young fellow whose only accomplishment was an ability to strum steel strings and pour out his heart in lonesome-sounding blue yodels?

Well, maybe he could get on, somewhere, with some other radio station. And even if his first record never got on the market, still—he had that contract! Even if it didn't mean much, it was something to show proudly; proof of—something or other.

At last Jimmie gave in to us; Lottie Mae and myself, and agreed that it was for our baby's good. Her grandfather, Aaron Rodgers, adored his Jimmie's child, and kindly Mother Rodgers, together with Lottie Mae, would give our Nita the very best of care. Most important of all, either there in Geiger—or in Meridian with my folks—our little daughter could be getting her education. Very soon, now, school would be starting.

So—it was decided that our little Nita should take the train for Alabama that very night!

Having made up our minds to let our baby go, there was, of course, much hurried unpacking and repacking to be done.

And right in the midst of it came a messenger boy with a telegraphed money order from my sister Annie, in Washington D.C. More money! Fifty dollars! In our

MY HUSBAND, JIMMIE RODGERS

possession now were seventy whole dollars!

To Annie I had explained our being headed for Bristol, and why; and had intimated, quite plainly, our desperate circumstances, in spite of our good hopes. So she wired us, urging us also to come to Washington, saying she was sure we could both get work there; she'd help us find it. Both? Yes, she knew, of course, of my short business course, and in my letter I'd told her of my determination to hunt work somewhere, whether Jimmie consented or not.

What we needed; what we had to have, regardless of what Bristol might mean to us, was some regular cash coming in every single week; if only a few dollars. Just something we could depend on. None of us had warm winter clothing. So—I was going to get a job. Mrs. Jimmie Rodgers was going to work; anywhere, doing anything, just so it was honorable—and meant cash. Now, my sister, Mrs. Alex Nelson, of Washington, was going to stand by us. She would help me persuade my stubborn, darling husband that it was wise and right for me to be a working partner in the firm of Jimmie Rodgers and Family.

Seventy dollars! Train for Washington—when? Early tomorrow morning. Train for Alabama—tonight. We were almost too breathless with hurried plans and excitement to think of grieving over the approaching break-up, even if only temporary, of our little family. Just the same, every moment Jimmie spent hovering over his baby; but being careful not to be sad. She shouldn't take our tears with her.

Suddenly, astoundingly, Jimmie said: "Throw your things together, kid. We're leaving here—for the big hotel!"

I stopped throwing my things together, looked at my husband and gasped. A room at the "big hotel" would cost us almost as much for one night as the one we now had would cost for a whole week! And we would be here only one night. Why move?

Jimmie's eyes and mouth were a little stubborn, a little guilty, as he turned to look through narrowed eyes toward those windows in Tennessee.

MY HUSBAND, JIMMIE RODGERS

Suddenly, I knew; knew exactly how he felt. At first this room had seemed pretty grand, after the cheap, shabby holes we'd endured "on the road." Now it was—depressing, somehow; made you feel cheap, frustrated, in prison; just a window, a door, four walls—.

Before I could say anything, Jimmie turned back to me, saying a bit defiantly: "I want to feel like somebody—just once more!"

Lottie Mae stared at the two of us, as suddenly I declared gaily: "Okay darling. You're the boss! Gangway—let's get going!"

"Well, my goodness! You kids!" said Lottie Mae Rodgers.

But—we were alive tonight; we had money! Seventy dollars! Never again, maybe, would we have that much, all at one time. Winter clothes? Perhaps we wouldn't need them. Perhaps we wouldn't be here. Who could tell? Who knows what will happen—tomorrow? But if a swell room, with private bath, in a nice hotel, could help my boy celebrate this momentous day, then that's what he should have!

And in the lobby of that lovely hotel I knew that not for one moment would I ever regret what that move had cost us—in dollars. At a time when, quite literally, we didn't know where the next dollar was coming from.

Watching my Jimmie, swaggering a little, but looking the picture of health, I was completely happy. His straw hat was worn with an air! His step was firm and confident. His eyes were bright. Yes—too bright and his cheeks too flushed. Danger signs, I knew, yet happy signs, too. Few could guess, I knew, watching him ever so closely, that the lungs under those bravely erect shoulders were so ravaged. Few could surmise the wasted-away body under that threadbare, yet somehow smart, summer suit. Happy! Just then, that was what mattered! I was frantic for him to be happy, content, just every possible moment of every day. There might not be very many of those days.

Yet, however content, neither of us could forget for one moment that our baby was leaving us—in just a little while now. And—when would we see her again? Ever?

We had no time then to dwell on that, nor even to enjoy the lovely room, so soul-satisfying after the one we'd just left. A door, windows, four walls—but what a difference! It had not only spaciousness and comfortable, even luxurious furnishings; it had—well, an air. You knew that it had welcomed nice people; people who were accustomed to nice surroundings. Somehow, a room like that can give a "lift" to the wanderer; especially to penniless vagabonds weary of heart as well as in body.

But—there's always the business of eating to be attended to. Back again we went to the modest little cafe on State Street where we'd coffee-ed up and asked about "the Victor man." The owner, to our delight, "made over" our child when he learned she was leaving that very night. He gave her candy bars and her favorite chewing gum, in return for which she informed him:

"Daddy phonographed today for Mr. Victor."

He pretended great surprise. "Is that so? Who is your papa? Do I know him?"

Miss Carrie Anita Rodgers replied importantly: "There he is. He's Jimmie Rodgers, national broadcasting artist! And he's my Daddy!"

Through her laughter Lottie Mae told Jimmie: "You'll never need a press-agent; not as long as she's on the job."

The depot! Never, whenever we had occasion to be in a railroad station, did Jimmie Rodgers fail to show eager interest. Unless too weak to walk alone, his step quickened, his very being seemed to expand with joy. His eyes would narrow with wistful longing to be not merely an onlooker, but once again a part of that surging movement. To be one of those blue-garbed figures, alert, vigorous, laughing or hurrying homeward after their day's work. The great, throbbing engines. The lights. People. People laughing—or crying; weeping with joy or sobbing, brokenly in grief. People confused or people sturdily confident. And people waiting; just waiting.

Soon now that southbound train would go speeding through the night toward

MY HUSBAND, JIMMIE RODGERS

Alabama, taking away from us—just about everything. Tumbled hair of gold, eyes deep blue and, almost always, filled with teasing laughter; tight-clinging jealous little arms; sturdy little whirlwind feet.

In the days that followed it seemed that our little family was continually having these enforced separations, but we, all of us, did our best about our good-byes. We tried to make them gay, but—.

So, this night in Bristol, waiting for that southbound train, Lottie Mae and I watched Jimmie and his little daughter together; Nita clinging tight to her worshipped and worshipping Daddy's slender, too-white fingers; Jimmie proudly, pathetically loading her with fruit, candy, toys, story books—Jimmie Rodgers and his baby girl—pretending to be gay.

As the train pulled slowly away from us we hurried frantically along beside it, following "her" window, and—just at the last—Jimmie crooned mischievously to his idolized little daughter and his well-loved sister: "You may see me—walking down the railroad track—You may see me—Oo-de-lay-ee. Whoo-whoo-oo—."

So, laughing back at us, waving, they vanished into the night. And we were alone. My feeble efforts at bright chatter met with but little response. Anyway, I didn't feel like talking, either—.

A real train had gone; quite different from the one that had so worried me—and still did—and this one bore precious freight—. Laughing words from Jimmie's long-ago railroad days came to me: "That old eight-wheeler may take a notion to leap the rails—."

I clutched my husband's arm and demanded: "Darling, sing! Sing to me as we walk along. Sing—."

Before I could think what I'd like him to sing, he was crooning so softly that not even the passers-by could hear:

"Sleep—baby—Sle-e-p—."

CHAPTER TWENTY-THREE

"I'll hush this song—

"That I never will sing—

"No mo', no mo', no more—."

"Hi, Jimmie!"

The eager friendliness of that, to me, strange voice succeeded in bringing us both out of our grief, our loneliness, better perhaps than anything else could have done just then.

There in front of our hotel stood a well-dressed man, his right hand out-stretched in hail-fellow greeting, his round face beaming. Instantly Jimmie gripped that hand, calling the man by name, and told him proudly: "I want you to meet my wife."

I learned then that he was a traveling salesman who had met "Special Officer" Rodgers in Asheville. He had, he said, just come from there. He told Jimmie: "Fred Jones says folks around there are anxious to hear you on the air again. I caught your program one night. You sang that—what's the name of it? The one about poor Thelma." He stopped to chuckle and added: "Boy, that's keen, believe me! And you can yodel! What are you doing now?"

Jimmie answered readily: "Well, I'm under contract to the Victor phonograph company. Just made a recording here today; and I'm going to be broadcasting again soon. Washington, D.C., I guess."

Jimmie never changed expression when I pinched his arm!

His friend said: "Well, say, that's fine. Phonograph records! I'll buy the first one I can find. I hope it's that one about Thelma."

My Jimmie said easily: "Well, no—it isn't. Savin' that for later. Next time, maybe."

"Under contract to Victor—." Well, I thought, amused, he's just telling the truth. It certainly isn't his fault if it sounds bigger than it is!

When his friend had hurried along to keep an appointment I teased Jimmie: "I love me!"

He grinned, and said suddenly: "I want some ice cream."

Perched on the stools at the fountain, Jimmie told me: "Shucks, Mother—might as well begin tootin' my own horn, if I'm going' to get anywhere. Can't afford to hire a fella to do it for me, like the big guys do. Just the same, I gotta be gettin' myself a name. That's what counts in this business. —Gosh! I sure gave that fella a sample of his own medicine. I mean, if he just knew about it, he got a lesson in good salesmanship. Well, all I got to sell is my guitar, my voice and myself. And I gotta be quick about it, too. —For her sake—our Baybo's—and for my mean mama's sake, too."

Jimmie lingered in the lobby of the hotel to glance through the late editions, but I hurried up to that lovely room, smiling to myself tenderly, thinking: "I bet he's hunting to see if the Associated Press wires are carrying the news yet—the news that Jimmie Rodgers has just made his first record for the Victor Company."

But, thinking of that record, of what it might or might not mean to us, my worries again gripped me. I remembered suddenly that he couldn't possibly know how the public in general would receive that "Soldier's Sweetheart" thing. He hadn't risked using it over WWNC! Why—I wondered. Afraid it would be jeered? Yet now—when everything in the world depended—why? Why?

So—there I sat on the edge of the bed, sunk in something like utter hopelessness, when I should have been proud and happy; when, too, I should have been enjoying to the fullest that grand room and the luxury of a hot bath!

I didn't hear Jimmie come in; didn't know he was there at all, until I realized he

Jimmie in one of his most famous (and stylish) publicity poses, showing off his Weymann "Jimmie Rodgers Special" guitar.

Top: On the patio of the Rodgers home in Kerrville, Texas, with wife Carrie,
eight-year-old daughter Anita, and Mr. and Mrs. Ralph S. Peer.
Bottom: Jimmie in his Sunday best at nineteen years of age.

"The best friend that I ever had." Jimmie
with his father, Aaron Rodgers.

Though his first recording contract was still six years away, Jimmie, in this portrait circa 1921, looked more like the "man of affairs" he would one day become than the railroad man he had always been.

Top: Jimmie again with Carrie and the Peers. Bottom: The Jimmie Rodgers Entertainers: Jimmie, in specs, with Jack Pierce (standing) and Jack and Claude Grant, WWNC, Asheville, North Carolina, 1927.

Kerrville, Texas, 1930.

Jimmie wearing his favorite hunting outfit, same locale.

As Carrie told Jimmie, "Unless you look well, you'll never in the world
have a chance to show what you can do."

Top: Jimmie with the Carter Family (Maybelle, A. P., and Sara) in Louisville, Kentucky, 1931, where they had just recorded "Jimmie Rodgers Visits the Carter Family" and "The Carter Family and Jimmie Rodgers in Texas." Bottom: Posing with fellow hillbilly star Clayton McMichen in Tupelo, Mississippi, December 1929.

Top: Visiting with Major Gordon W. Lillie, better known as Pawnee Bill, and
Lillie's wife at their Oklahoma trading post in 1930.
Bottom: In January 1931, Jimmie toured Texas with humorist Will Rogers.
Here they are in front of Blue Yodeler's Paradise, Kerrville.

Always ready with a smile, a song, and a hat, for any occasion.

Another publicity shot with the Weymann guitar.

"In those days," Carrie writes, "about every six months, I think, Jimmie bought himself a new car!"

A movie still from *The Singing Brakeman*, the Columbia-Victor Gems short Jimmie made in 1929.

Carrie and Jimmie at Monmouth Beach, New Jersey, in 1932,
the year before Jimmie died.

The Singing Brakeman.

"Thumbs up on the spot!"

was standing right there in front of me, close, and doing something mighty odd, to say the least! With middle finger and thumb he was flipping something—a hornet, maybe—off my shoulders; first one, then the other.

"Jimmie! What—what is it?"

As if he hadn't heard, he hissed softly: "Scat!—Scat!"

I started to get away from there, hurriedly—but Jimmie warned: "Whoa! Wait a minute! I'm scattin' those devils off your shoulders, Sugar. Two of those little gloom-devils—squattin' right on your shoulders. One—right there—shoo; an' one—right—there—scat!"

Suddenly my boy-husband's thin face wore a huge frown. He doubled a fist and shot it at me threateningly, as if he meant to—bust me on the nose. Astonished, indignant, I drew back—and that doubled fist was firm under my chin—gently forcing my head up—up—and my boy was laughing down at me—whispering a gay: "Chin-chin, Mother."

It had been a long time since that threatening fist had shot at me, like that—since I'd heard that gay "chin-chin." But then—I always tried never to let him catch me harboring gloom-devils. I'd always do some quick scattin'—when I saw him coming.

So now—I did my best to give him a little keep-up-your-chin grin. At which my Jimmie chuckled, pulled my hair and "whoo-whoo-ed" and I was ashamed.

In this moment, this grandest day of his life, perhaps, when my love and loyalty—and gaiety—should have been on tap to help him enjoy it richly, to the fullest, I was failing him; had failed him—by not attending to that scatting myself; by forgetting to chin-chin.

But in spite of his scatting, in spite of my shame, I just couldn't seem to be rid of those gloom-devils; although I tried to make my smile—honest.

Jimmie tried to comfort me then: "She'll be okay, Sweetheart. Bet she's sleepin', sweet an' pretty, right this minute. Fine train, that is. Got a dandy crew, too."

Just a moment before I had been bent on loyalty, gaiety, for his sake. Now, almost hysterical, still thinking about that other train that had gone, I wailed: "It isn't Nita, this time! It's—it's Thelma!"

His sudden yowl of glee was good to hear—even if I was almost in tears.

He told me then: "I know what you're thinkin', Sugar—but I'm goin' to show you where maybe you're wrong. I know what I'm doin'. At least—I think I do—." He stopped there to chuckle. "Gosh, Honey, you sure tickled me today, buttin' in like you did up there at Peer's. I sure got a big kick out of it."

Indignant, I said: "Well, Jimmie Rodgers! When I was only trying to—."

"Now, wait, Hon. Don't go gettin' all darkened up like that. Honest, Mother, it was swell of you, tryin' to help put all this over for me—. My wife fightin' for me—tryin' to make the man let me make another record so I could do 'T for Texas,' Well, look Carrie, all this means a lot to me—more than even you can guess, maybe. Because of what I'm goin' to do for my two girls some day.

"But, here's the idea. When Victor's deciding board listens to my record I want 'em to get the music! See what I mean? Want 'em to be able to judge the quality of my voice and my playin'; I mean the way I try to make the guitar strings a part of my voice; make 'em say what I do and feel what I do. And when they're listenin' I want 'em to be able to make out what I'm sayin'—without havin' to think about it. I don't want the words, themselves, to get all the attention.

"If I'd given 'em Thelma some of 'em would be surprised, some shocked and some tickled; but there wouldn't be any of 'em, maybe, stop to figure out whether I really had a voice or not, and maybe they wouldn't even know I'd played a guitar. They'd all be thinkin'—well, about me shootin' poor Thelma. Those fellas up there, they're bound to be more critical than radio listeners–in. Maybe they'd like Thelma—maybe they wouldn't; but I'll make a guess they'd think maybe the public wouldn't."

"But the public did like it, Jimmie."

"Yeah, I know. Maybe I'm wrong, givin' 'em just sweet, plaintive old-fashioned things. But if those fellas up there at the factory are smart, like I think they are, they know that's the kind of stuff the public's ripe for, right now. Folks are about fed up on smart alec jazz and jungle stuff. Well—if they do happen to like me—my voice and my playin'—and these pretty, old-fashioned numbers, why then they'll have sense enough to know I can put over all those old hill-billy things, sentimental or rowdy."

"Yes, but Jimmie—your blue yodels."

"All right, Hon. S'pose I'd given 'em Thelma and they'd okay it. See what'd happen? Next time they'd want some more of the same; and the next, and so on. I've got 'em all right, but I haven't got 'em all worked out good yet. I need somebody to help me. Got some dandies in the back of my head—railroad, hobos, barroom; and got a lot of ideas for pretty, sentimental little things, too. Just, wait, Sugar. You'll see."

I was beginning to see.

He added: "Anyway, I did some yodeling today. Yeah, I know. Not blue ones; just the same I've done my best to make 'em softer and prettier, make 'em mean more than other yodelers do."

Thinking of his lullaby yodels, tender, crooning, I was, at last, comforted; the little gloom devils had scatted. And I saw what I had forgotten temporarily; that Jimmie Rodgers was nobody's fool. Happy-go-lucky as he always was, the good things of life didn't just happen to him. He made them happen, by shrewd planning and by stick-to-it-iveness. Bad things had happened to us again and again. But the bad things were, I knew, mostly the fault of that old enemy of Jimmie's which he somehow couldn't seem to lick a standstill: That old T B.

So, at midnight of that marvelous day in Bristol I cold-creamed my face, yearned for my baby's arms, and heard my husband singing softly to himself while he made ready for the luxury of a steaming bath: "I've got a barr'l of flour—O, Lord! I've got a bucket of lard——." The song snapped suddenly. I heard a splash and immediately a startling: "Whoo-whoo-oo——. Gosh! That water's hot."

Laughing, I warned: "Hush, darling. Folks are asleep."

Then came, very softly: "Sle-e-p——Ba-a-aby——Slee-ee-p——."

CHAPTER TWENTY-FOUR

"You got me worried—

"But I won't be worried long."

At that time, despite his jaunty effort to "keep his chin up," Jimmie Rodgers was a very sick man; for all I knew—dying. You can't tell about T B, especially if you are unable to provide constant medical examination and treatment. He could have neither—at that time.

He needed not alone sympathetic, understanding companionship; he needed, constantly, painstaking personal care. No matter how courageous his bearing, how ambitiously eager for accomplishment, there were times when even so small an effort as preparing his own bath would bring on such a distressing spasm of coughing that it seemed his very life was going—.

He needed somebody to take from him, as much as possible, the little pesky worries of just plain, everyday living—to post letters, run little errands. Too, whenever possible, he must be persuaded to take long hours of rest daily; complete relaxation of mind as well as of body. He must have, when possible, tempting, home cooked food. He must be saved from exposure to dampness, chill and cold. Ravaged lungs weaken a body and make it easy prey to other diseases, especially pneumonia.

At that time there was absolutely nobody except myself to do those things for my boy, and I wanted to do them. I was thankful I could be with him; and that I had strength and health to run and fetch and carry.

107

MY HUSBAND, JIMMIE RODGERS

It was as much as I dared wish for, just then, to see those whimsical smiles on his lips, to hear those impudent snatches of teasing song, to know the crushing sweetness of those jealous arms; to watch, on occasion, the confident swagger of that slender, boyish person who was my husband, Jimmie Rodgers.

I was afraid. Afraid he would not—could not—live through that winter. When spring came—.

I was still more afraid when we definitely turned our course northward, and left Bristol for Washington, to seek shelter with my sister, Annie, and her husband, Alex Nelson. This welcome "invite" would, we knew, give us a breathing spell while we set about the business of getting back on our feet.

And in Washington, almost immediately, I had two battles with Jimmie Rodgers! It was all I could do to hold out against him.

No, I shouldn't work. Please, please—just give him a little time. He'd get us back on our feet; making a living for us. That was his job, not mine. His playing and singing would bring in the bacon. And as soon as his record got on the market—. Just give him a chance to book himself some dates as a single entertainer, a chance to get himself on at one of the broadcasting stations. He wasn't going to have his wife making the living—not as long as he could stay on his feet!

So—I found myself in the position of the surgeon who must be cruel to be kind. Annie and Alex backed me up. Was I or was I not a partner in this firm? Of course he'd provide for us; would make money soon—gobs of it. But why couldn't I be doing just any little old thing to bring in a few dollars each week? Just to tide us over. Help get winter clothing.

But even with the stout support of my sister and her husband I could not make Jimmie see it my way, this business of his wife working for wages.

Annie had a government position and was teaching in a business college nights. She managed to find me a position as stenographer with a law firm—and I lost my nerve! My short business course was so far in the past I realized I couldn't embarrass Annie or myself, or take up an employer's time with my incompetence.

Then, making the rounds, Jimmie got caught in a heavy downpour and came home soaked to the skin. By night he had a high temperature and was bedfast for days. That collapse sent me, post haste, for a steady job just the moment he was able to be up and around the house.

Marvelously, it seemed to me, came the chance to work in one of the "Happiness" tearooms. It meant a uniform; meant being on my feet long hours. It meant also the embarrassment of accepting tips—but how that embarrassment faded and how thankfully they were pocketed when I thought of my sick husband and my precious baby a thousand miles away from my arms!

Still—it also meant nice surroundings, dainty foods temptingly arranged, and nice people—cultured, low-voiced people. It meant splendid treatment from the management; and more than all, it meant—weekly wages, steady and sure.

Jimmie knew I'd been working—and for wages, but I think he had not quite believed it until the moment when he sat there on the bed in our room, staring at my wages—and tips—which I had thrust into his hands. And I sat staring at him hoping, fearing.

He had "darkened up" instantly, but before the storm broke I, quite unashamed, resorted to woman's tried-and-true weapon, tears, and conquered him. Conquered him, but never convinced him. He was of the same opinion still about Mrs. Jimmie Rodgers working for wages. Throughout the ensuing months he never gave up trying to persuade me to "quit it."

Then came our second battle. That when I attempted to point out to him the necessity of his making a prosperous appearance there in Washington if he expected to be engaged as an entertainer at smart clubs and various social events. Or even to be taken on at a radio station.

MY HUSBAND, JIMMIE RODGERS

The prime reason for my argument, of course, was to provide him with thick wool clothing for the cold fall and winter. He needed just everything; a good wool suit and overcoat, gloves, muffler, overshoes—and, if I could persuade him to wear it, a fur cap with ear-laps!

As I told him when he started storming: "Listen, darling. Don't worry about me. That wool dress I had last winter is just like new. My work doesn't call for anything real swell, and they furnish my uniform. But it's different with you. Unless you look well, you'll never in the world have a chance to show what you can do."

Jimmie just growled: "Don't need 'em. I'm a railroad man. Makes me no never mind. But you—you've got to have a warm winter coat."

"But, Sweetheart," I protested. "I don't have to be out in all kinds of weather making the rounds. My spring coat is plenty warm enough—over my good wool dress."

I neglected to tell him that, while the good wool dress was plenty warm enough indoors, by the time I'd got to the tearoom mornings, even wearing my spring coat, my bones were nothing but blue goose-flesh. Nor did I tell him that just that morning, when I'd hurried to get into my uniform, one of the other girls, all bundled up and snug in furs, had exclaimed: "My goodness, Carrie! Aren't you freezing in that thin coat?" To which I had laughed and responded: "Well, I'd be completely frozen without it."

So the battle raged between Mr. and Mrs. Jimmie Rodgers—about warm winter clothing, but at last I won out. Chiefly because he failed again and again to find anybody willing to engage an unknown entertainer who claimed he could play a guitar and yodel, and who showed a few fan letters—and a "contract."

A theatrical agency got him a few cheap dates out in the suburbs, playing as a fill-in between pictures in neighborhood theaters. But sophisticated Washington refused to be bothered with him. It wouldn't even listen long enough to learn whether or not he really could provide entertainment.

MY HUSBAND, JIMMIE RODGERS

So—at last Jimmie Rodgers had to admit I was right, pocket his pride; acknowledging that, no matter what you have to sell, if the buyer looks down his nose at your shabbiness you've lost the sale before you've even had a chance to display your goods.

But in spite of his finally being so well outfitted, that Washington winter almost proved fatal to him. It was tough on us both, neither of us having ever known really severe winters, with deep snow, thick ice and freezing air that made one gasp. To one in Jimmie's condition it was fearful. It was all he could do often to fill an engagement when he succeeded in getting one. Still, now that he was "prosperous," he was beginning to receive better dates.

Even so, money—actual cash—was still mighty scarce for us. It seemed some way, that the more we made between us, the more places there were to put it. Therefore, I felt that I just had to keep right on working, and as long as I did, Jimmie refused to pass up any date that meant a few extra dollars, no matter how badly he felt.

One morning he lay moaning and writhing in pain; a high flush on his cheeks, his lips white and drawn, grim with the effort to choke back his groans. Pleurisy, this time. Well, we needed cash so badly I felt I had to go to work. We couldn't afford to lose even one day's earnings. Still I was frantic. He'd need me there. I wanted to be there. But I had to work. I couldn't—we couldn't—.

And Jimmie insisted stoutly, in spite of his sufferings: "Don't worry about me, Mother, I'll be all right. Goin' to get up from here pretty quick now. Got that luncheon date this noon. It'll mean several hundred dollars. Gotta have 'em."

It was getting late and there was no time to argue. I called the doctor. He said he'd be right out. Then I phoned the theatrical agency: "Mrs. Jimmie Rodgers speaking. Jimmie's sick in bed. No, he won't be able to fill that luncheon date. Sorry."

When I called back from the tearoom later there was no answer. No answer all day. Well—the doctor had been there, had eased him and now he was resting comfortably; was sleeping. I didn't worry—much, but I hurried home as fast as I could.

As soon as I was safely out of sight that morning, Jimmie had called the doctor and told him not to come. Then he'd phoned the booking agency that he would fill the luncheon date, and phoned the drug store to send him up a plaster.

"Daggone it, Mother. Think I'm goin' to stick in bed, helpless and useless, while my wife's on her feet all day long—pocketing tips? Not on your tintype! Here."

Proudly then he poked into my fist the first few dollars he had earned that noon and which meant so much to us!

But Jimmie Rodgers, confidently expecting a call for a second recording, was "eagle-eyeing" all letters received at the home of Annie and Alex. He fairly haunted the telegraph offices. And almost daily he reminded Long Distance where he could be reached.

"I don't understand it, Mother. Looks like I'd be hearin'."

Still—no word of any sort.

I noticed then that he was developing an unaccustomed habit. Floor pacing! Accompanied by huge frowns of puzzlement. He couldn't figure out what was wrong. Had something he hadn't foreseen gone haywire with his hopes and ambitions? Something that might completely upset his plans for our security? And—if so—what could he do about it?

Well—he'd do something. He wouldn't stay in the dark. Not Jimmie Rodgers!

Then, during one of my off-duty hours I slipped home to find him—not pacing the floor, not frowning, but—strumming his old guitar and caroling lustily:

"I smell your bread burnin'—turn your damper down—If you ain't got a damper—turn your bread around—O-de-lay-ee—."

CHAPTER TWENTY-FIVE

"Sleep—Ba-a-by—Slee-ee-p—."

Something had happened!

Down in Dixie Land the Williamson tribe, including all the in-laws; the Rodgers tribe, and their in-laws, and Jimmie's own mother's folks, the Bozemans, all rubbed their eyes, caught their collective breaths, and couldn't believe it. Some strutted, and some wept—with joy.

Over in Geiger, Alabama, Lottie Mae Rodgers bragged: "I told you so!" Mother Rodgers wore a pleased smile, and Aaron Rodgers, Jimmie's beloved Dad, sat huddled in a rocker, salty tears running down his worn cheeks. Then he hurried to bring in his cronies to share his joy, to spill to them his pride. In other words, to do some tall boasting!

In Meridian the neighbors hurried to the Williamson home to learn what on earth was wrong. They'd heard laughing, crying and singing—all at the very same time.

On a street corner, near by, my baby sister, Mildred (Mitchie), lingering with her little friends after school, suddenly "lifted her ears," then emitted a loud yelp and went racing homeward, squealing: "Carrie and Jimmie's home!"

All of this excitement down in Dixie was caused, of course, by nothing more nor less than some black discs. The home folks were hearing once again the plaintive, silvertone voice of their Jimmie, crooning an old-fashioned lullaby and his little war song about his buddy who'd given up his life in France. So they listened—and listened again.

And was there was any excitement, and rejoicing, in Washington? Well, just a little—even if the bulk of Washington knew nothing about it.

We had the house to ourselves. I think we danced a bit; madly. I know we laughed and cried; first one, then the other, then both together. Then we fell silent—just listening.

Presently I realized that Jimmie Rodgers, sitting there beside me listening to his own voice singing "Soldier's Sweetheart"—well, his eyes were a little moist. Gently I asked: "Darling, what is it?"

For a moment he couldn't speak. Then—he told me: "I was just thinking—'bout Sammie and Nettie—."

Not until then had I dreamed that perhaps Jimmie had—a bit hesitantly offered this simple little ballad to the world as a splendid tribute to his before-war-days pal and that pal's sweetheart!

Through the living room window, then, we saw Annie coming home. Hastily Jimmie reset the needle so that just as she was entering she heard her brother-in-law singing; heard his voice—yet there he stood, not singing at all. Just smiling a little—watching her. Just waiting.

Annie squealed: "Jimmie! It isn't true!" Then my sister had my husband in her arms, hugging him tight, kissing him, laughing, crying heartily.

For many weeks I had great difficulty getting to work on time or getting back home promptly. I was a very busy Mrs. Jimmie Rodgers. Busy following that beloved voice. I just couldn't resist hurrying forward, retracing my steps, or going out of my way—when I heard its clear, sweet tones. If it came from a residence or apartment, I'd stall along or walk back and forth, until the folks inside must have thought that woman out there was crazy, or something! If it came from a dealer's, I'd just stand there, outside, until the last golden note had trailed into silence.

But Jimmie was the practical one. If he lingered in the various music stores, it was not to listen proudly to his own voice, but to get some idea of how that black disc was selling. It had to sell. Had to click with the public—or he could not expect a call for a second recording. And if he never got that—where, then, was our security?

He told me one night, worriedly: "Don't seem to me like it's going so hot, Mother. Gotta give it time, maybe."

I said: "Why, Honey. Seems to me like it's being played everywhere. That means— it's selling! You mustn't expect too much of it—just at first! Anyway, it's bringing your name to public notice."

Jimmie grinned: "Well—I just hope 'Mr. Victor' gets busy and takes notice." He added, frowning a little: "Just one record isn't going to bring home much bacon for us. If I don't keep 'em rollin' out I'll never get anywhere. Funny I don't hear. Looks like they'd send me some kind of word."

Poor Jimmie! His thick, warm clothing failed, that winter, to prevent his having numerous set-tos with just about every sickness in the list: Flu, grippe, pleurisy and one siege that seriously threatened pneumonia.

Now that it seemed we might be in Washington indefinitely I had been so wishing we could have our Nita with us. But I just couldn't bear the thought of her making such a long train trip all alone, even if we could spare the money for her fare; or even if some of the railroad members of the family could get her a pass. Too, I hated to take her out of school. She'd have to start all over again, there in Washington, and in the middle of the first semester.

To both Jimmie and myself, this matter of seeing to it that our little daughter got a proper education was something of a problem. It seemed we'd never have an established residence. The poor baby seemed likely to get her education in "smatters," as her Daddy had—wherever a schoolhouse was handy.

Her letters, in childish scrawl, came regularly. But now, after she'd heard her Daddy singing—and he wasn't there at all—came a letter in which the words themselves sounded brave—but with baby longing and loneliness everywhere between the lines. It was quite the longest letter she'd ever managed, with faulty spelling and writing not true to line.

As Jimmie and I together read that pitiful little letter, we could just see that sweet, solemn face, with hair of gold tumbling into, no doubt, tearful blue eyes.

"Dearest, dearest Mother and Daddy, Daddy and Mother." (Doing her best to put neither of us before the other.) "I go to school every day. I like my teacher. Grandma and Grandpa and Mitchie and all of them are good to me. I love them all and my little gray cat. And the blue plaid dress you sent me. I hear Daddy on the phonograph. I guess it's pretty but I don't like it very much. I'd rather see you, Daddy, Mother, Mother, Daddy. Are you coming home soon? Your love, loving, lovingest daughter, Anita. x x x x x x x . P. S. I can't make as many crosses as I have kisses because I haven't any more paper in my tablet."

Not much of a letter to bawl over, perhaps; but both of us went around all that evening trying to wink back tears that refused to stay winked back.

Jimmie said: "Let's send for her."

It was all I could do to sob: "No! No, Jimmie. We've got to let her stay in school. She's got to get on with her education."

And that night I had a request to make: "Please—please don't play—'Sleep, Baby, Sleep!'"

That was, of course, the cue for my loving husband to take me in his arms and try to comfort me, but he did nothing of the sort. He gave me one distressed look, grabbed his hat and coat—and beat it, muttering: "Gotta see a fella."

I didn't ask him where he was going. Anyway, I wanted to be alone. I had a letter to write, to our child, explaining as well as I could why we couldn't "come home." That, and so many other things.

Then, quite suddenly, I was in the arms of my husband. They smelled of sweet, fresh night air, mingled with the rich fragrance of cigarette smoke. Those sensitive fingers were teasing a strand of my hair and my ears were hearing a soft: "Whoo-whoo-oo—oo-de-lay-ee."

CHAPTER TWENTY-SIX

"My baby, I know that you want me—

"Each lonely night and day—

"Your dear blue eyes, how they haunt me—

"Though you are far away—."

Jimmie was still in the dark as to what, if anything, Mr. Peer or "Mr. Victor" was going to do about him. I think he began to fear that perhaps he'd used poor judgment. Perhaps he should have given poor Thelma a chance. Maybe he'd never be able now to surprise and delight a vast public with those doleful blue yodels. Perhaps he'd be shelved for all time.

From the distributor and the various dealers in and around Washington he learned that his one-and-only record was having a more than fair sale—for an unknown. If that was true in Washington, it seemed bound to be true, more or less, throughout the United States. Yet—no command for a second recording. No telegram, no long distance call, no letter; not even a penny postal.

Jimmie restrained his impatience about as long and as well as he could manage; but he wouldn't stay in the dark forever. He wanted action!

He told me: "I'll give 'em three days more. If I don't hear by then I'm goin' to New York to see Mr. Peer. Reckon maybe he's forgot me. No use writin' him. I can talk to a guy better—face to face. He's a nice fella—but I reckon he's just too busy, maybe, to remember me."

"If you think it's anything like that, why don't you just catch the first train in the morning? I've got some money saved up. A little. Enough to help pay your expenses."

MY HUSBAND, JIMMIE RODGERS

Jimmie frowned a little; then he grinned: "Well, Sugar, might be I'll have to get a loan off you, just temporary. I—I had to put out a little, couple days back."

"Shooting craps?" I teased.

He started to say "no," but changed it to: "Well—maybe."

Well! If Jimmie Rodgers had lost some money gambling, that was news!

But Jimmie was saying: "Nope. Can't leave tomorra. Got an appointment real early in the mornin'. Don't you try to get up and fix and breakfast, or even coffee for me, though. You pound your ear just as long as you can. I'll get my coffee outside."

Almost every night my last conscious thought was a prayer for my baby, so very far away from my arms; and every morning I'd wake up—missing her so terribly.

That morning when Jimmie Rodgers left me pounding my ear while he hurried away to get his coffee and keep his appointment, I struggled back to consciousness—with my precious baby's arms tight around my neck!

Laughing, crying, all three of us at once. I had time to remember, just the same, that this was why Jimmie had to "put out a little money, couple days back." This was his early morning appointment.

But when I learned she'd made that long train trip alone, mother-fashion I had a lot of worrying to do—even though my baby was safe in my arms! But my husband and my child both assured me fervently that it was a beautiful train and a grand Pullman and that just everybody on the train had been "just fine" to her.

Breathlessly, then, our small daughter told us: "I told everybody on the train about my Daddy phonographing for Mr. Victor." She added with a note of disappointment: "But most of 'em already knew about it."

Three days. Three grand reunion days for the Jimmie Rodgers family!

Then there was the matter of getting our daughter started to school there in Washington; and the exciting business of getting Jimmie off to New York—to "talk to a guy, face to face."

MY HUSBAND, JIMMIE RODGERS

First, of course, there were earnest discussions of ways and means. He had enough cash to get there, but would not have one penny for hotel or other expenses. How could he get back home—if he failed in his mission? What if he should get down sick again?

But, just then he was feeling fine and looking better than for a long time; so we didn't mention that—except that I made him promise to "take it easy," rest all he could and not worry. If things went wrong; if he found he needed more money or needed me, he was to let me know. I'd arrange some way.

I made him take my small savings—ten whole dollars. He finally consented to take it "temporary," but he was pretty rebellious about it.

Grinningly confident as always, when our Jimmie kissed us goodbye he asserted: "Just you wait. I'm goin' to give 'em 'Way Out on the Mountain' and 'T for Texas.' Thelma's goin' to have her chance to help bring home the bacon; help put us on top of the world. And she will, too."

We let him go, Nita and I, both of us smiling and calling after him: "Good luck, darling!" And Jimmie called back, elated: "Two of 'em! From my two! Gosh—now I know—."

The winds whipped away his last words, but we could see him leaning out to grin back at us, his beloved old guitar held with both hands high over his head—as a promise to "his two."

CHAPTER TWENTY-SEVEN

"When the north winds blow we are goin' to have snow—

"And the rain and hail comes boundin'—

"I'll wrap myself in a grizzly bear's coat—

"Away out—on the mountain—."

I was made aware many, many times during my thirteen years with Jimmie Rodgers—and even before—that his was a unique personality in more ways than one. Over and over again his daring, his defiance of established custom, his impudent disregard for the "expected," together with that take-a-big-chance gambling spirit of his, made me gasp.

I think the average young man in the precarious position in which Jimmie Rodgers was then; an unknown, knowing that "my time ain't long," that sooner or later that old T B would get him down, would have sort of tiptoed most cautiously into the great, rushing city of New York. Especially if he was a "furriner" from the Deep South, a lanky nobody who had something less than ten bucks in his jeans to pay for room, meals and other incidental expenses, including a doctor, maybe.

However, my Jimmie got himself located satisfactorily; then proceeded nonchalantly to get Mr. Peer on the phone.

He told Mr. Peer casually that he just happened to be in the city (!) and would very much like to make another record—if he could use another at that time—!

Mr. Peer was a busy executive—and is. He is also a kindly person with a clear understanding of human nature. But had he, his mind so fully occupied with various other and more pressing matters, just sort of let this boy slip his mind? Or was he, as well as the RCA Victor Company, merely awaiting full and complete returns on that lone Jimmie Rodgers record? Even if this beginner looked fairly promising, did they—all of them—consider that there was "no hurry, plenty of time"?

But with Jimmie—"Gotta be quick about it—."

When Ralph Peer heard, over his telephone, that drawling Mississippi voice casually advising him that Jimmie Rodgers was still available to make another record, I've no doubt he could see, in memory, that shabby, lanky youngster with his pitiful cough and wistful smile. Jimmie Rodgers, he'd said his name was, and he'd had his wife and little girl with him—a penniless itinerant musician, stranded there in Bristol.

And when he answered, I suspect a sympathetic little smile was hovering around his lips; for underneath that painfully casual drawl he must have sensed the repressed eagerness, wistful longing—even fear.

So he told Jimmie Rodgers: "Why, yes. I think we can use it now. I'll arrange it. We'll have to take a run over to the factory, in Camden. Where are you stopping?"

To which came the astounding reply: "Me? I'm hotelling at The Menger."

Little wonder Ralph Peer gasped. The Menger. Now renamed th Hotel Taft. One of the finest hotels in New York City.

When Jimmie told me about it later, his brown eyes twinkling, I listened in amazement.

"You see, Ma—I just naturally like the best; and I believe in taking it."

"Yes—but Jimmie!"

"Aw, shucks, Mother—I knew they were payin' for it." Again I gasped, remembering he'd known nothing of the kind! They would; yes, if they accepted him for a second recording. But—at that time they hadn't said they would. Hadn't sent for him!

"Anyway, I figured they were a powerful firm and wealthy, and I was one of their artists. Course, they'd want me to do 'em proud—so I did."

After Mr. Peer had consented to another recording, if Jimmie Rodgers could possibly have managed it in those brief hours before "taking a run over to Camden," I am quite sure he would have made a hurried round trip by air to have spilled me his grand news. Messages of all kinds, including a long, long special delivery letter, did come breezing into Washington to "his two." And the burden on them all was "now will you quit it?" And, as always, at the bottom of the last page of every letter, down in the lefthand corner, was: "Be true to me, Sweetheart—'cause I love you."

Does that little message read as if my Jimmie were jealous? Well—he was. Perhaps nobody except myself could read and understand the plaintive pleading behind that little message which he never failed to add to his letters to me. Had he cause? Well, this is what he told me: "Sweetheart, during all our years together, you've never given me the slightest reason to be jealous. But—I just can't help it. It's just—'cause I love you so."

Now would I quit work? No, I wouldn't. I didn't. What if that first record was selling? We had seen no cash from it yet. What if he had made a second recording and had given Thelma and the blue yodels a chance to keep us from starving? They might bring us in a few dollars—six months from now.

But not around thirty dollars in cold hard cash every single week-end!

Frankly, while I hoped for the best, I just didn't have his faith; although, of course, that was my most carefully guarded secret. To me, it couldn't be true—that ease and comfort might be heading our way. Nothing could be more true but poverty, debts and sickness. Never enough of anything. Nothing good could be true, except that we had our baby with us—and that my boy was so eagerly confident—so happy.

Yes, I'd lost even my faith in Thelma and in the blue yodels. The train had gone.

But in Camden, Ralph Peer had arranged for his new protege, Jimmie Rodgers, to "make another record." And had escorted the young singing brakeman to—of all

MY HUSBAND, JIMMIE RODGERS

places—an old church! There, easily confident as always, Jimmie had strummed his old guitar and sung: "Where the snakes are vile—and the zebra grows wild—and the beavers paddle on walking canes—."

Also, there in the Trinity Baptist Church, long since abandoned as a place of worship, but through the doors of which many of the greatest musicians of the world had slipped in and out, Jimmie Rodgers crooned and moaned: "I'm goin' to buy me a shotgun—with a great long shiny barr'l—" and on until the last blue yodel of "T for Texas"—to go on the market as Blue Yodel Number One—trailed into silence.

CHAPTER TWENTY-EIGHT

"I woke up this morning—

"The blues all 'round my bed—."

We didn't have a blue Buick. We had another second-hand Dodge. More foolishness, perhaps, considering our still almost penniless condition and our debts. But we'd both felt we needed a car for transportation; especially for Jimmie to get to his various suburban dates without having to stand around in cold wind, rain and sleet. So—when we'd found what we considered a real bargain, Sister and her husband, Alex, bought it for us. That is, we expected to repay them, of course, some day. But I know they never expected to live to see the day.

So in our second-hand Dodge, back Jimmie Rodgers came from New York—jubilant. New York was great. Peer was a swell guy—a regular fella. Swell bunch at the factory, too. But doggone, he'd felt funny, he said, whangin' his old guitar and singin' his kind of stuff in a church—where there'd been hymn-singin', and preachin' and prayin'. He reckoned maybe the Lord didn't mind, though, since He'd never sent a bad storm to destroy it.

The Trinity Baptist Church in Camden has won its own niche among the renowned musicians of the world. It was built for religious worship in 1872, but had to be abandoned because it was not built right. The acoustics were all wrong. Yet, strangely, it proved to be one of the preferred recording studios of the world; its acoustics perfect for that purpose. It is said that, to this day, acoustics engineers are mystified and unable to explain why this should be so.

Through the doors of this old church-building, since acquired by the RCA Victor Comapny for use as a recording studio, have passed such world-famous figures as Stokowski, Kreisler, Galli-Curci, Ponselle, McCormack, Toscanini.

Sir Harry Lauder recorded here; and lost a treasured tobacco porch which, it is said, he considered had been stolen—and in a church!

Here also came popular crooners; among them Gene Austin to give to a delighted public his famous "Blue Heaven."

And here now came an unassuming unknown, Jimmie Rodgers, ex-brakeman, soon to surpass them all in sales; soon to top the lists of Victor best sellers—and to hold that position throughout his career, rivaling the sales of the greatest tenor of all times, the beloved Caruso.

Yet, when he returned to Washington, beyond the fact that he had been permitted to make another record he had little reason to be so jubilant, so far as I could see.

But he told me that Mr. Peer had urged him: "Give us your best, Jimmie. The professional life of a recording artist is never more than three years. Give us your best."

That seemed to give Jimmie much confidence. I supposed he took it to mean a foregone conclusion that he would be allowed to continue making more records—for at least three years.

Ever since we had been in Washington, Jimmie had been diligently, if offhandedly, spreading the news that he was a "Victor recording artist." He could do that with good face, since his one lone record was sort of backing him up with its steady sales. And now he had actually made another record!

Before I quite realized it, my Jimmie had become more and more a popular entertainer; welcome even among the professional musicians, even if he didn't know one note from another. He was excited, happy, contented, about his growing popularity—which meant a little bacon—about what he considered our excellent "prospects," about everything—except his wife working for wages—and tips.

Still I refused to "quit it." Always in the back of my mind were terrifying little pictures. When spring comes—if that old T B—if anything happens—.

Then Jimmie told me: "Goin' to get my first royalty statement pretty soon, now, Sugar. Get 'em quarterly, you know. Then you'll see!" He yodeled at me gaily, and added: "Pretty blue Buick for a pretty mean, blue-eyed mama."

Just wait! You'll see!

The royalty check came—and I saw! Twenty-seven dollars and some odd cents!

Three months' royalties!

If three people had to live three months on nothing more than twenty-seven dollars and some odd cents—.

No bacon there; not even the rind. If I had not been working. If he had not been getting dates more readily now!

And Jimmie? Well, it was a bitter blow to his professional pride. His high hopes for our future—for that yearned-for security—came crashing around his ears. Just for the moment he, too, lost faith in Thelma and the blue yodels. With those vanishing lungs he couldn't hope to go on forever playing club dates—or even broadcasting.

He was a weary, unhappy figure, his long length stretched out on the bed, his cheeks wearing that angry flush, his brown eyes so puzzled—so distressed.

I knew that, given a few moments, he'd rally out of it, find a cheerful grin, reach for his guitar and strum and sing his way to new and perhaps better plans; but I couldn't bear to see him so—the blues all 'round his bed.

In the best "natural" voice I could manage, I told him: "But look, darling. They tell me it takes maybe, six months or more to really get over unless you've already got a following, like you'd have if you'd ever worked in vaudeville or musical comedy. The only following you have is the home folks, and the folks around Asheville and those mountain resorts. Lump them all together, wouldn't be over a thousand, maybe; and part of them family groups. Not over three or four hundred to actually buy records. See?"

But it was hard for him to see, just then. He was too bitterly disappointed. He muttered: "Looks like I was dead wrong about it. You were the wise one. I ought to have given 'T for Texas' the first time."

I had to do some quick about-facing. I told him, stoutly: "You were right your ownself! I—I've changed my mind. It's just like you explained it to me there in Bristol; maybe you'd never have got a chance to make another record, at all—if you'd given that rowdy 'T for Texas,' first time." And I forgave myself that little white lie—when I saw how it had cheered him, even though he didn't believe a word of it!

He sat up, got a cigarette going, and grinned at me.

"Thought I'd found my alley, Mother. Still think so. But—doggone—it sure is slippery!"

CHAPTER TWENTY-NINE

"She's long—she's tall—

"She's six feet from the ground—

"She's tailor made—

"She ain't no hand-me-down—."

So—in our pathetic ignorance we did our best to console each other and to defy a destiny which seemed to have in store for us nothing but an uncertain and rather desolate future.

But—what a celebration we would have that night if we had had any suspicion of the truth!

If we could just have known, as we were told later, that that measly twenty-seven dollars and some odd cents represented the largest royalty statement ever sent out to a beginning solo artist on the Victor lists!

But, unknowing as we were at the time, we would have had a pretty skimpy Christmas if it had not been for Sister and Alex and the homefolks. Always, all of them had been so wonderful to us; stood by us so unselfishly, so loyally, throughout all our struggles, without hope—or hint—of their generosity ever being repaid.

Yet, for all our disappointment, our dashed hopes, there wa no denying that we were much better off that Christmas season than we had been for several years; since we'd been married, in fact. Jimmie's various engagements were fairly steady and well-paying, we thought; and my wages—and tips—were at least steady.

And then my boy's spirits—and mine—soared high. A call! And he had not gone after it! A formal notification direct from the factory, to be there in the studio in

MY HUSBAND, JIMMIE RODGERS

Camden at a certain hour of a certain day.

Jimmie Rodgers was there on time.

As in New York, so in Camden. Jimmie had told me: "I like the best—and I believe in takin' it. Anyway, they're payin' for it." So straight he went—to the Walt Whitman.

Jimmie Rodgers didn't know—and wouldn't have cared—that this was contrary to all custom; especially for struggling beginners and even for most of the old timers on the Victor payroll. And thereby—it seems, he caused something of a flurry among the Victor officials. They were, quite naturally, amazed—but they were delighted. Here was somebody different. A personality.

Then, very soon after his return, came his second royalty statement.

Around four hundred dollars!

Well—that was decidedly different! If we could have four hundred dollars instead of twenty-seven, coming every three months, besides what we were both earning otherwise—well, we certainly could get along fine!

In truth, his blue yodels were already—as we were more or less aware—"sweeping the country like a prairie fire." His first record had set the blaze; and now "Away Out on the Mountain" and "T for Texas," his second record, were spreading that blaze with astounding rapidity.

My own darling husband a celebrity; a sensation!

It just didn't seem true!

But—he was on the air over WTFF, and was now being advertised everywhere as "Exclusive Victor Recording Star" and "America's Blue Yodeler" and also as "The Singing Brakeman."

It was Ray McCreath, at that time announcer over WTFF, who suggested the title "America's Blue Yodeler" for Jimmie. It was used thereafter in all of Jimmie's publicity matter put out by the Victor Company, as well as by Mr. Peer in the song albums, using Jimmie's numbers exclusively, which he later published and put on the market.

Now came urgent calls from the factory: More—more—more—.

And suddenly Jimmie Rodgers discovered that, for all his shrewd planning, for all his keen forsightedness, he'd made one rather bad slip-up. He had somehow never gotten around to bringing all those "dandies" in the back of his head to the front. Now he couldn't supply the demand fast enough! He was forced to "dig"; to appeal to others to dig—for old out-dated numbers which he could bring to light again, revamp and make his own.

But what he needed to do, of course, was work out his own "dandies"—for the sake of the added royalties that would be his, as lyricist and composer.

"Gotta have somebody help me make some sense out of 'em. I've got the titles, and the ideas—got some of the phrases and melody worked out—but I need help."

So—he rushed off frantic word to the Williamson family poetess: Elsie McWilliams, his sister-in-law. Elsie scurried to Washington, bringing with her all the sweet, ancient ballads and quaint ditties she could find in the stacks and stacks of old, once-popular sheet-music at Mother's. Bringing, too, some of her own little verses which, as a more than capable musician, she had set to music.

And the music-factory started. Day and night; night and day. Snatches of this and that; whang—twang—strum—some words—more words. Repetition to drive a bystander mad!

Mrs. Jimmie Rodgers continued working—for wages and tips. Perhaps because she was wound up and couldn't stop perhaps because it all seemed like some fantastic dream. Pretty soon she'd wake up and find it wasn't true. Nothing could be true—but poverty—sickness—.

For all his continuous whanging of his beloved—and now famous—guitar, for all his varied exciting activities, Jimmie found time to be devoted and sweet; and to urge, over and over again: "Please, Sugar—will you quit it?"

Ray McCreath resigned as announcer for WTFF, planning to take the new celebrity on his first "personal appearance tour." But before actually beginning that tour Jimmie wanted to take Elsie to New York for a conference with Mr. Peer. She must have a share of the royalties; she should have a contract.

It was arranged for the three of them to head that way. Ray McCreath, as Jimmie's booking-manager for "the road," would contract theater dates along the way, put out advance publicity and have the house managers on their toes so that, when the dates were played, they'd be assured of turnaways. Then Jimmie and Elsie were to hurry back, grind out more numbers for future recordings, and be in readiness to answer the next call.

And then, while that New York trip was being planned so excitedly, came for me about the most difficult decision I ever had to make, I think; to resist stubbornly their insistence on my going along. I had an almost childish longing to go—but it would mean quitting my job. I might never be able to get it back. I—we—might need it. So I refused even Jimmie's pleading.

Resisted, even when he teased wistfully: "Girls all 'round me by the score—guess I could claim a dozen or more—but I want nobody but you-oo—."

When that lonesome sounding bit of song trailed away to a whispered: "Please," I was still shaking my head.

And Jimmie told me in song: "I'm leavin' you, mean mama—just to worry you off my mind—yodel-aye-ee-del-ooo—."

CHAPTER THIRTY

"Got the blues like midnight—

"The moon shines bright as day—

"I wish a tornado—

"Would blow my blues away—."

So away they went, in our old Dodge. The three of them; Ray McCreath, Elsie—and my husband, Jimmie Rodgers, with "success" in capital letters now firm-grasped in those long too-thin white hands of his.

And I watched them go, sending them on their way with my gaiest smiles—and winking back childish tears that stung my eyes.

They'd have such a good time! It would be such a lovely drive! I was young and longed to be in on all the fun and excitement; yearned to go places, see things, do things with the rest of them.

Well, it was my own fault—afraid to quit a job that might not be waiting for me when I got back. But—we might need it so! And Mrs. Jimmie Rodgers hurried back down to her work, her job in the tearoom, worried about being a few minutes late.

That very evening, when I'd got home feeling so terribly restless and forlorn, a fifty-word telegram arrived—commanding!—me to drop everything, take the first train for New York. Complete instructions were included—but no explanation as to "why."

Had all the excitement and activity gotten my Jimmie down, at last? Another hemorrhage? He'd had none since that terrifying time in Meridian. If one now—wouldn't it be fatal? The yellow slip was signed "your Jimmie"—but anybody could have written it.

Frantically I phoned the teamroom; told them I'd return the uniform later. I was told: "Please keep it. If you can't come back steady, come back extra. We'll have a place for you."

New York. Everybody rushing. Everybody happy—or so it seemed to me.

I was thrilled, overjoyed to see my boy looking so well, so full of high spirits, his two arms tight around "his two." But—why had I been sent for?

They were, both of them, Sister Elsie and Jimmie, so glad to see us—as if we'd all been apart for months! Aside from that they were—well, they just simply overdid their matter-of-factness. Something was in the air.

Busy unpacking, freshening myself up to "go eat and take Nita to Coney," thrilled with our lovely room at the Menger, I kept demanding: "Why? Why did you send for me? I had to quit my job! Might never get it back. What is wrong?"

Jimmie Rodgers, grinning from ear to ear, no matter how hard he tried to hang onto his poker face, told me: "Aw, shucks, Mother. Can't I have my two—my wife and baby—with me once in a while? Come on, let's get going."

I tried to protest that Nita ought to be made to take a little nap first—and that I felt the need of a brief rest before going to eat, and to Coney Island, but I got exactly nowhere—.

Jimmie simply grabbed me by the arm and dragged me down to the lobby, Elsie and Nita following.

Mechanically my feet headed toward the coffee shop, but Jimmie steered me away, and I protested: "Where are we going? I thought we came down to eat."

"Not here," Jimmie said casually. "It will be more fun to eat at Coney."

To the garage then, to wait as patiently as we could for our car. I watched every one of the long stream of cars coming down the ramp, hoping that each would be ours—our second-hand Dodge.

MY HUSBAND, JIMMIE RODGERS

Suddenly Jimmie was saying: "Told you I would, Sugar—some day."

With a wide sweep of his arm he was indicating something coming down the ramp—"something new, something blue."

Mrs. Jimmie Rodgers stared, unable to believe. If given a few seconds' time she would have spilled her tears all over the blue cheviot shoulder beside her, not caring if all New York saw—and snickered.

Jimmie Rodgers, "Exclusive Victor Recording Artist," gave his wife no time for weeps. With great ceremony, but equally great dispatch, he handed me into that proud, gleaming, shining, brand-new—blue Buick. Ours—at last! Our dream for seven desolate, weary years—come true!

"Just you wait, Sugar. I'll get it for you—some day."

Several days in New York. Business finished, and then, speeding madly back to the Capital City; proud, happy—thrilled in our grand blue Buick.

Hurrying back—to find an urgent call to Camden.

Not one record, just two numbers, to be supplied this time. But twelve!

I bundled my uniform under my arm and went back to work—for wages and tips. Even though America's Blue Yodeler, already so beloved and already getting bundles of fan mail, gloated: "Now, Sugar, I guess you'll quit it."

But—I just couldn't quit it! Not just yet. Even though Jimmie's records were selling like wildfire we had to wait for those quarterly settlements before we actually had the cash. We needed, just then, every single dollar we could scrape together. His royalties, his earnings in addition to them, and my earnings—all, every penny aside from actual needs, must go into the bank; then be checked out again, immediately.

Debts. Debts that had piled up for years. Most of our creditors, I know, had never expected to see a penny of what we owed them but we were giving them a surprise.

"Darling," I told Jimmie. "What I earn will pay our living expenses—the household expenses and help with the clothes—and the rest, what you make—."

"Sure," Jimmie said instantly. "Those debts must all be paid. But please don't worry, Sugar. I'll pay 'em off. Not going to have anything like that hanging over us any more—if we can help it. But I'm making plenty. No need for you to keep on working now—even if you did think so once. Maybe—I shouldn't have bought—."

Laughing, I put my hand over his mouth: "Don't you dare say you shouldn't have bought our blue Buick. I'd keep working ten years—for wages and tips to help pay off those debts—just for the—the knowing our dream could come true—."

Well—I couldn't let him worry, even if I did realize that what he'd paid for "our dream" would have taken care of most of our obligations. Anyway, his next royalty check would more than square up everything. He'd been so little-boy pleased, surprising me that way—when I'd never suspected a thing! And I was just as little-girl pleased—loving that beautiful car—crying with happiness and pride to know his first thought had been to keep a promise he'd made way back in Meridian—.

Besides—even yet my Jimmie's success didn't seem real to me. It just couldn't be real. In fact, it was many months before I could bring myself to spend as much as five whole dollars for something which was not an actual, pressing need and even then, not when I could get something almost as good for one dollar.

Not until the time came when Jimmie's royalties mounted, with startling speed, to an average of two thousand dollars a month could I bring myself to give up my pathetic little job—which I might never be able to get back!

The call to Camden. Twelve numbers; not just two.

But Jimmie and Elsie were all set. They'd been working like mad. Now they were all packed to speed to the factory. There would be the business of completing arrangements about her contract—which Jimmie insisted on, even though Elsie kept saying: "Now Jimmie, what I really want most—is just to see that you get over, and to help any way I can. I'm not thinking about my part of it. Just too glad to help—"

Jimmie grinned: "Reckon you could use a bit of extra cash, though, couldn't you,

MY HUSBAND, JIMMIE RODGERS

Sister?"

Elsie laughed: "Can't we all? Yes—maybe it would be kind of nice—if I could do something extra for our children.

Jimmie told her: "You bet. Three grand youngsters. Bet Dick's havin' himself a time with 'em—without their ma there. Bein' a police, though, he's got his club."

So—laughing, they told us all: "So long. Be back before you know it."

And at that moment a message from Meridian was put into Elsie's shaking hands.

Her little Patricia, her beloved eight-year-old, was seriously, dangerously ill. Poor Elsie—our hearts ached for her. We comforted the distracted mother as best we could. It seemed there was nothing to do—except fly home to her little one—.

She said pitifully: "Jimmie-boy—it looks like I've got to let you down. I—I've been so anxious to help you—."

Jimmie said promptly. "Don't worry about that part of it, Sister. I know what it means—to have your little one down sick—and be miles and miles away—."

I knew he was remembering, too, what it means to lose that little one and have not one dollar to contribute toward buying a little casket.

Jimmie was telling her, his arms tight around her: "Look, Elsie. Here's what we can do. We can start on to Camden and I'll wire Dick before leaving and at every station along the way, so there'll be word for you at every stop. Then if—if little Patricia is worse, I'll put you on a fast train for Meridian. Our Master up there is kind. He'll understand."

Elsie McWiliams dropped to her knees—and prayed; prayed earnestly to her God, through her tears, to spare her darling and to allow her to stand by her beloved young brother-in-law, who needed her so badly just now. She told her Lord that if he would just grant her this one blessing she would give her church every single dollar of her first royalty check.

By the time they reached Camden little Patricia was, miraculously, it seemed, entirely out of danger. The crisis had been passed. Her precious little one would live. God had answered her prayer.

When business arrangements had been completed to everybody's satisfaction, Elsie told of her promise to God.

Smilingly sympathetic, somebody suggested sending her first royalty in two checks, one to follow a day or two after the first.

But to Elsie a bargain was a bargain. She wouldn't cheat God. When her first check came she kept her promise; gave every single penny of it to her church—three hundred dollars.

And at home, during a few off-duty hours, I was making a trip to town with Annie—on the street car. It was crowded and we had to strap-hang. Above our bobbing, swaying heads the advertising panels caught our eyes, and held them.

There in one of the nicest panels, the picture of our own Jimmie laughed down on us—his hands resting lightly on that old guitar, and in fat, black letters: "Jimmie Rodgers, Exclusive Victor Recording Artist, America's Blue Yodeler."

Laughing excitedly we climbed off that street car, leaving our Jimmie's likeness to go on making the rounds—while we proceeded with our exciting dime-store shopping.

And we heard, here, there and everywhere, it seemed: "I'm goin' to shoot poor Thelma—just to see her jump and fall—O-lay-ee-o-lay-ooo—."

CHAPTER THIRTY-ONE

"If you ever had the blues—

"You know just how I feel—."

Fourth of July week, 1928. Blues! We had nothing else but! Not my happy Jimmie's sobbing-throated blues, although they assailed our ears from every direction, nor even little gloom-devils to be scatted.

Up the Potomac, which I am sure must have been a bright and shining blue that day, came a gleaming little yacht, wearing proudly a two-word name; two words which were on the smiling, singing lips of many, many thousands of folks throughout America.

There were, of course, other golden throated singers besides my husband. Others, even on the Victor lists. Others crooning gay, appealing little ballads—"My Blue Heaven."

So the dainty little yacht, *Blue Heaven*, sailed proudly up the Potomac to the Capital City bearing its young owner, Gene Austin, his wife, pilot, manager, and his Filipino chef.

In our beloved blue Buick, with another car loaded with guests following, we drove as proudly to a point near Gene's *Blue Heaven*. Myself in cool, thin blue for that July day; Jimmie natty in white flannels—and wearing his railroad watch and chain.

Out we scrambled with our contribution to the party; a dozen fried "springs."

We had our springs—and many other things—on deck, buffet style. Before which Gene made a formal speech of thanks to Mr. and Mrs. Jimmie Rodgers for the hamper of fried spring chicken, and wound up with:

"But everybody lay off the gizzards. All of 'em. They're mine." They were. Gene Austin gobbled every single gizzard from all twelve chickens!

But Jimmie was more than content—if he could have all the drumsticks he wanted.

Watching those two that day was, for me, pure joy. Two young business men already amazingly successful, earnestly discussing the various angles of show-business, of selling entertainment. Two young married men, devoted to their families. Two boys, almost irresponsible they seemed, wise-cracking us into stitches: Gene Austin and Jimmie Rodgers, recording stars.

And—watching my happy boy that day, I was suddenly fiercely glad for all that success meant to him. Because he belonged to me and I to him? For those two reasons, naturally, I was intensely proud and thankful. But apart from those two reasons I was fiercely glad for him—as a human being.

Knowing his story as nobody else, until now, ever has really known it, I couldn't help feeling that no human being ever deserved to win through more than did the section-foreman's little boy, the cheery-hearted young brakie with melody in his Irish heart, the devoted husband and father battling that old T B. Being downed again and again by bitter poverty, sorrow, heart-breaking disappointments—yet refusing to stay down. Stoutly refusing to admit defeat; his gay banter, his wistful grins, his bits of rollicking song ever giving himself—and others—courage to stick and win through. "Trust me, Carrie. I'll make good—some day."

The blue yodels weren't starving us to death. We need never again, perhaps, consider feathers for food. Ambitions realized were doing wonders for him physically, too, it seemed. It had been a long, long time since I'd seen him looking as well in every way as he was in the days of that glorious summer of '28.

But—when the excitement began to be an old story, would it—could it last?

Watching him, laughing there with Gene that day, I saw that his laughter was bringing on another spasm of coughing—distressing, agonizing.

Perhaps, now that we could afford it, I could persuade him to take a good, long rest—in some sanitarium high in sunny western mountains where he could sit long hours in the sun. Nothing to do no—pesky worries—.

And then I heard Jimmie telling Gene about the string of dates Ray McCreath had lined up for him: Annapolis other places. And he was going to see his old Dad. And—and—and—.

No. Jimmie Rodgers, of the restless feet, could never sit in the sun with folded hands for long hours, days, weeks, months.

I realized, somehow, that no blue heavens over sunny western hills could be more healing, could better prolong that precious life, than this blue heaven which he had created for himself and his two. Happiness, contentment, freedom from those aggravating worries. Doing what he loved best to do, and being paid for it.

Add to this the knowledge that even though his old enemy, I B, continued to dog his steps, he could still be in the game; the grand, bustling, hustling game of Life—of living, of accomplishment.

That day I realized that my husband, Jimmie Rodgers, would continue his wistful, rollicking minstreling until that day when his Master would tell him:

"Lay aside your old guitar, Jimmie. Come to me—and rest."

Driving home that evening, tired but happy, Jimmie grinned:

"Twenty miles to a yodel, Ma."

As always, then, he broke into a bit of caroling, "making up" words and music as we sped along:

"Got myself a pretty mama in blue—and a blue Buick—and we'll never have the blues no mo'—Yodel-ay-ee-ee—Whoo-whoo-oo—."

CHAPTER THIRTY-TWO

"I'm thinking of you tonight, old pal—

"And wishing you were here—."

Just a few months ago that joyous day on Gene's *Blue Heaven* was recalled to me—as well as a later occurrence, about which Jimmie had told me.

In the cabaret scene of a Joan Crawford picture Gene sang something about—old pal. Perhaps he was not remembering Jimmie just then, but suddenly I could see the two of them laughing together. And I could see them, also, having a hilarious time—as Jimmie had told me—in a palatial hotel in Florida, trying to "separate" a twenty-dollar bill. They wanted some change; neither had anything smaller than that twenty. It was more fun to have a friendly fuss about it than to phone down to the desk for change.

The twenty refused to "separate" and at last Gene settled the matter. He tore the bill in two—let the pieces flutter to the floor and very elaborately washed his hands of the whole matter. Suddenly the hilarity became almost shamed silence. Quietly Gene gathered up the pieces of silk-threaded paper and thoughtfully fitted them together.

What memories Gene had I don't know; but Jimmie was remembering—many things. Remembering our Nita's little bank with three thin dimes for breakfast, remembering a little white casket and no money to pay for it, remembering, too, a yellow twenty placed in his hands in Bristol, and what that twenty had meant to a shabby, almost desperate young man.

Gene said quietly, but with a little smile: "Going to see if I can darn the darn thing together—and keep it as a souvenir." So—watching lovable Gene in that Joan Crawford picture I couldn't help wondering—if he still had that "darned" bill and if he remembers Jimmie sometimes when he sings about—old pal.

Poor Sister Annie and her husband Alex had been nearly driven out of house and home that spring of '28 when, almost overnight, their young brother-in-law had become a celebrity. Gobs of mail, messenger boys, phone calls, callers professional and otherwise, to say nothing of the music-factory!

No need now for us to impose longer on their kindness and generosity. So at last we found a cozy furnished cottage. Although I longed to just settle down to some nice housekeeping for a while—I kept on working—for wages and tips.

But at last I yielded to Jimmie's insistent: "Please quit it, Sugar." I quit it, content then to be just Mrs. Jimmie Rodgers. And immediately found myself involved in other work besides housekeeping, exciting work; playing secretary to America's Blue Yodeler. Fan letters to answer, photos to package and post; contracts and statements to file; books to keep.

When Jimmie's records first topped the best sellers on the Victor lists—as mailed to all distributors and dealers—the distributor for that district handed one of the lists to Jimmie, saying: "Better frame this, boy. Keep it to show your grandchildren. It may never happen again."

But it happened continuously—over five years. Until his death and even after. Yet Mr. Peer told him that the professional life of a recording artist is only three years! Incidentally, Jimmie Rodgers was the first solo artist to be advertised "alone" by the Victor Company.

Not even the constantly growing popularity of radio could stop the phenomenal sales of Jimmie Rodgers' records. Not even the storing of talking machines in attics and barns, nor the sensational new "talkies." Not even the Great Depression.

One of the reasons for this was the many "publics" Jimmie Rodgers could reach. Family groups delighted in his sentimental ballads. The poverty-stricken, gripped by sickness and troubles almost more than they could endure, knew that here was a fellow who understood; who had "been there." Far, lonely cabins on western plains, on the high ranges, in distant forests; isolated dwellers in such places knew that this boy knew them, too.

Railroad men and their families thrilled to his songs of the silver rails. Army men—hard-boiled, grim-faced he-men—scoff and wisecrack though they might, knew deep in their hearts a genuine liking for "Soldier's Sweetheart." As did members of the American Legion. For sailors and their sweethearts he crooned and yo-deled: "Dear Sweetheart—as I write to you—my heart is filled with pain—for if the things I hear are true—I'll never see you again—."

Even the "rowdies" in poolrooms and barrooms—yes, he knew them, too.

He talked the language of all of them. Sweethearts—mothers—fathers—hobos—husbands and wives—even cops! For each, some gift of cheer, of sympathy, of broad or tender humor. Jimmie Rodgers reached them every one with his sobbing, lonesome yodels; held them with his whimsy, with his deliberate audacity.

Cops the country over chuckled when he moaned: "Police—police—police—you're just as drunk as me—!" And "We both drank lots of liquor—that flat-looted cop and I—I thought he'd never leave me—Lord!—I thought I'd die."

And—frail, wasting-away human beings, desolate in various stages of the grim White Plague? To those the gallant voice of Jimmie Rodgers brought not hushed, "long-faced," avoiding words—but boldly flung defies, and cheer-section razzing for their common enemy, that old T B. Ring-fighters know well enough that the surest way to confound your opponent is to razz him. Moreover, it does something to you, yourself; gives you added strength and will to stand up and take your punishment—with a grin.

To one not a member of the world's T B clubs, that "T B Blues" of Jimmie's sounded—well, sad, depressing and not a little shocking.

Such a subject wasn't to be mentioned in public in such forthright fashion. It was indelicate—almost indecent.

But to the "lungers" it was, according to their own appreciative letters to my husband, a greater tonic than any physician, any specialist, had been able to prescribe.

They needed—just that! They realized that his gay wisecracking had in it nothing of "grim humor." It was—their own language; the language of tubercular patients in any sanitarium— if no outsider is present.

So—they chuckled: "Old boy Jimmie! He knows!" And their chuckles were good medicine.

When he followed with "Whippin' That Old T B"—those who had managed to fight through this far, but were, perhaps, on the edge of despair, eagerly renewed their battle. Again letters came pouring in, from near and far, telling their minstrel, their Jimmie, all about it.

Another, and very large public for Jimmie Rodgers, one may be certain, consisted of humble, less-fortunate strugglers with stringed instruments; all diligently listening to his records by the hour—trying to find out, if they could, how he got that way.

That July day, in '28, Gene Austin had told Jimmie: "No use wasting your time working shotgun and neighborhood houses. Just as well be working the big ones. Seating capacity is what it takes; and you can fill a big house just as easy."

Jimmie was, of course, anxious to cash in on his popularity while he had it. He figured the public might—just might—tire of him pretty soon, no tellin' when. Maybe he was just what showmen call a "freak," a novelty that would wear out. But the thought of working the "big time," even though he was already a real celebrity, had never occurred to him.

Gene got busy. The Earle, in Washington, was running stage shows and feature pictures. The manager of the Earle was a personal friend of Gene's. But, he protested, he already had his headline act booked for that week. Like to oblige a friend—but—.

Gene has some stick-to-it-iveness, too! He told his friend: "All right. Book Jimmie as a Special Added Attraction. I'm tellin' you, man, he'll wow 'em!"

So—the singing brakeman, the long-legged Mississippian with his Deep South drawl, his unassuming ease of manner, his wistful charm, got his date at the Earle to headline the bill—the first week in August, 1928, exactly one year from Bristol.

One year—from a stranded, shabby nobody—to a headline position in a large city theater, and to an average of two thousand a month in royalties from his phonograph records!

For all my Jimmie's composure in whatever surroundings he found himself, I rather think he was—well, a little uncertain when he went backstage at the Earle that first day. No wonder. Gene had mysteriously absented himself when the time neared for Jimmie's rehearsal with the orchestra.

Jimmie was thoroughly at home backstage in shotgun houses and even in the somewhat better neighborhood theaters, but to the unaccustomed the regions backstage in a "real" theater are just plain scarifying. Especially when a rehearsal or performance is on.

Previously, the houses he had worked were, more or less, one-man affairs; being essentially picture theaters. Little attention was paid to such things as scenery, props and electrical effects. There were no stage crews, no maze of cables, no flymen, no battery of spots, no grips and carpenters, no harassed stage manager. When such a house booked an act, it might be the operator, or maybe the bill poster, or even the housemanager himself who'd attend to the business of supplying the performer's needs.

The Earle was different! Jimmie Rodgers wasn't nervous, wasn't an amateur, but everything backstage at the Earle was decidedly new to him—and everybody backstage knew it! They "ganged up on him."

"What kind of props do you use?" one shot at him.

"Don't need any," Jimmie drawled comfortably.

"Well—what do you have with you on the stage?"

"Just me and my old guitar."

"Any furniture?"

"Yeah—you can bring me a chair."

"No props at all?"

"Nope. Nothin' but a chair—to prop my foot on."

"What kind of a chair?"

Somebody, somewhere stifled a suspicious snicker. Jimmie Rodgers became aware of twinkling eyes. He drawled: "Aw, shucks. Quit your darn kiddin'. Gimme a box."

There was delighted laughter. But—they weren't through with him. The head electrician wanted to know:

"How about lights? Foot and borders full up? Any spots?"

There was a little hush. Perfectly at ease, Jimmie Rodgers lighted his cigarette and told the seemingly-worried juice man:

"You can just gimme a coal oil lamp, son. That'll do."

He was one of them! Jack Pepper was master of ceremonies for the Earle. He took the young phonograph star under his wing, gave him good professional advice, oiled the works for him.

And then Gene Austin showed up—grinning hugely.

In blue brakie garb, including the peaked cap, the blue bandana and the watch and chain, Jimmie Rodgers, boyishly slender and unassuming, gave to the patrons of the Earle his "T for Texas" and "Soldier's Sweetheart," together with other numbers. For his encore he gave—"Frankie and Johnny"!

In those days you didn't sing "Frankie and Johnny" in polite society nor in public to a mixed audience. So—Jimmie Rodgers did.

You sang it in furtive places, with a dropped eyelid and insinuating innuendos. So—Jimmie Rodgers didn't.

He gave it to the Earle with exactly the same earnestness, the same heart-throb sympathy that be had put into "Soldier's Sweetheart."

The "singing brakeman" took sixteen curtain calls.

Jack Pepper insisted Jimmie could have had a hundred.

But, my Jimmie was near collapse. Those sick lungs demanded rest.

"Root-to-toot—three times she shoot—Right through that hardwood door—She shot her man—he was doing her wrong—."

CHAPTER THIRTY-THREE

"I may be rough, I may be wild—
"I may be tough, and counted vile—."

Jimmie Rodgers was now a celebrity. Everybody wanted to know all about him. There was so little about him that anybody really did know. So—in no time at all "everybody" knew so much about him that wasn't so, that never had been so, and that was never to become so.

On a pleasant day in that first "miracle" year of ours, Jimmie came up to our room and said, amazed amusement in his voice and eyes:

"Well, I'll be dogged, Mother. Know what they say about me? They say I'm a rounder!"

I said, with a little smile: "Well, Honey—aren't they right?"

Jimmie thought that over for a minute; dropped into an easy chair, strummed his guitar lazily, then said: "Yup. Reckon so—reckon so." His fingers flashed across the guitar in a sudden gay, defiant discord; his eyes twinkled, and he said, with small-boy impudence: "Too bad!"

From babyhood, almost, Jimmie Rodgers' companions had been boys and men; boys and men of the railroad yards. Most of them honest, straightforward and scorning sham and pretense. The men were hard workers; substantial citizens, devoted family men. During their recreation hours they tossed their rye neat, flicked cards, rolled the ivories, told ribald stories. They got into arguments often settled by blows, after which strong hands gripped, glasses were bottomed-up, the air was cleared and the men were pals. These, then, were young Jimmie Rodgers' associates; the sort of men—he-men—he was at home with; rough and somewhat tough, perhaps—but never vile.

It was only natural when "fortune smiled on him," when business and professional contacts threw him among men who wore their Sunday clothes from Monday to Saturday, that he sought for his boon companions the type of men be felt "at home" with; even though they were politicians, legal lights, hotel owners, stage artists; even though they drove fast cars, were at home in gay restaurants and roof gardens; had luxurious quarters in swell hotels and clubs, or possessed splendid homes of their own. They were, like his former railroad buddies, men—he-men—who scorned pretense, sham.

If "rounder" means a man who has been around—then Jimmie Rodgers was a rounder. And if being a rounder made of him the devoted, considerate young husband I knew, and the tender, adoring father our little Anita remembers, then I'm proud that he belonged to that tribe of good fellows.

My acquaintance with so-called rounders may be limited; but of those I've known as such, never a one of them but was loyal, big-hearted, square; with open hand and purse, and a toe ready to boost his fellow man up instead of to kick him down. Any man who lacks those qualities isn't good enough to be a rounder; he's a bounder. There's a difference.

I shall always be thankful that I had the good sense, or intuition, to refrain from trying to make my husband, Jimmie Rodgers, over—after I became his wife. It was that debonair, yet shy and sensitive spirit of his with which I'd fallen in love. And that dauntless spirit could so easily have been broken by constant fault-finding.

Men of Jimmie's type, with his zest for living, may pretend to mock at sentiment. Yet they are, I think, the most truly sentimental of all men. And, at heart, they are deeply religious, I believe—even though some of them, perhaps fearing ridicule, may deny it. Their happy-go-luckiness is a sort of shining armor, perhaps, shielding their emotions; protecting sensitive heart strings.

MY HUSBAND, JIMMIE RODGERS

I remember, on a late afternoon some two years before my husband's death, the two of us were driving from San Antonio back to our home in Kerrville. On a hill-top, Jimmie drew to the side of the highway and turned off the ignition. Together, in silence, we feasted our eyes and hearts on the beauty of the most breath-taking sunset I've ever seen.

Presently Jimmie said: "Doggone it, Mother—it makes me want to cry." And he added scornfully: "And some folks try to say there's no God!"

Jimmie Rodgers made his last recordings with almost his last ounce of strength. Almost his last words were these: "I don't want to die. I've got everything in the world to live for; my baby, my wife and too much yodeling to do. But—if my Master up there calls me—I'll be ready."

Jimmie was religious; yet he professed no creed. He was not a church-goer; yet he chose for his wife a girl who was the daughter of a minister of the Gospel. He sang rowdy as well as sentimental songs; and the recordings of most of them were made in an old church building in Camden.

As a reckless young brakie on the New Orleans and Northeastern he delighted his rough and rowdy crew buddies with his rollicking songs; and as America's Blue Yodeler he delighted some sixteen hundred church folks one Sunday morning in Miami, with the same rollicking ministering.

When he had been brought back to Meridian for his last long rest, his body lay in state in the Shrine Temple; yet the final services were held in the First Methodist Episcopal Church.

Thus, churches and churchfolk entered the life of this non-church-going young brakeman again and again.

To some close friends of ours I once heard Jimmie say:

"Maybe God doesn't think I'm hopeless. I believe in Him. He don't have much reason, I reckon, to believe in me; but maybe He does."

CHAPTER THIRTY-FOUR

"But I found out last Monday—

"That Bob got locked up Sunday—

"They got him in the jailhouse—

"Way down town. He's in the jailhouse now—."

Regarding Jimmie's revival of those old songs of American ballad fame, such as "Frankie and Johnny," "He's in the Jailhouse Now," and others, reviewers the country over marveled because of his ability to take those old standbys and make engaging novelties of them. He made them "come into their own."

In Miami, when the Men's Bible Class—one of the largest in the United States—requested Jimmie to entertain them at their Sunday morning service in the Olympia Theater, Jimmie felt highly honored; but he also felt highly agitated.

He told them: "But I don't know any church songs."

"That's all right, Jimmie," they replied. "Give us anything you like. We're all anxious to hear you in person. Just sing your own songs."

So Jimmie Rodgers gave them "Jailhouse" and they liked it. But then, they liked him, that audience of more than sixteen hundred. It must be, as Jimmie chuckled to me once: "If they like you when you're nice, they'll forgive you when you're naughty."

Some of Jimmie's songs were naughty—but his candid, unfurtive rendition of them robbed them of all offense.

"Jailhouse" was, for Jimmie, such a surprise hit everywhere—even though it had been done for years—that Mr. Peer urged him to work out an original along the same lines for a "Jailhouse Blues Number 2." Jimmie did—in about twenty minutes; in fact, while we were waitingfor breakfast to be sent up in a hotel in Hollywood. He had it ready for recording the next morning, using the portable equipment Mr. Peer had brought to California for him.

Ralph Peer and the Victor Company arranged over and over again to take portable equipment to any place where Jimmie might be. He was valuable to them; and he was a sick man. His strength must be conserved if he was to continue turning out records for them. This arrangement saved him many an arduous journey. It also enabled him to fulfill his vaudeville engagements.

Jimmie had the true artist's ability of making any song that appealed to him decidedly his own. He made Kelly Harrell's "Away Out on the Mountain" famous. With Raymond Hall he worked out the first of the "T B Blues." And made that famous. His later gallant defy to his grim enemy, "Whippin' That Old T B" was his own.

"Ben Dewberry's Final Run," by Andrew Jenkins, won its way into the affections of Jimmie Rodgers' admirers. Waldo O'Neal's "Hobo Bill's Last Ride" he liked to sing because it gave him a chance to make his famous train whistle several times.

During that summer of 1928, there in the Capital City, when Jimmie Rodgers was just making his first "break" into big-time houses, he decided that his old "old guitar" sort of needed fancying-up a bit, maybe—if it was going into big-time show business.

But the large guitar manufacturing companies persuaded him to a different view. He must have a new guitar, with all the latest gadgets. They vied with each other—Weymann, Martin, Gibson—to persuade this boy, this yodeler who could take steel strings and make them a part of his golden voice, that he should use and feature their products.

He tried them all; liked them all. Although he admitted to me in a later year, that somehow the Martin seemed to "fit" better. It was to his Martin that he loved to turn to soothe him through a trying hour.

He made arrangements with the Weymann factory, of Philadelphia, to use, exclusively, a splendid guitar which they built for him as the "Jimmie Rodgers Special." This instrument, gold inlaid, with mother-of-pearl, this fifteen-hundred dollar guitar, was indeed a joy to behold. On its face was "Jimmie Rodgers," in pearl letters. When he'd finished his act and was taking his bows, he would suddenly reverse the guitar, and there on the back, also in pearl letters, was "Thanks."

Exhibited in the display windows of music-stores throughout the country, this beautiful guitar caused its own sensation, wherever Jimmie Rodgers appeared.

He liked the Gibson, too. It was "a sure-'nuff guitar and one anybody could make music with," he said. His mandolin and banjo were Gibsons, and he also owned several excellent Gibson guitars.

Still, it was the Martin that he loved. That was his "old guitar"—no matter how many new ones he owned. It was the Martin that "went into the mike" with Jimmie, whether on the road or in the old church in Camden.

A columnist once wondered why Jimmie Rodgers seemed to have won wider acclaim, as an entertainer in person, throughout the southern states than in other sections of the country. This is not hard to understand.

There were three excellent reasons. First; Jimmie Rodgers was a true-born Southerner, a native Mississippian. Second; he troubadoured constantly his love and longing for the Southland—the Carolinas, Tennessee, Mississippi, Alabama, Georgia, Texas. Third; his strength for arduous vaudeville engagements, requiring four performances daily, was not equal to the task. His three tours over major circuits all happened to be in the South.

But he was unable to make the tours which had been arranged for
him through the northern states and Canada. Had he been physically able to make those personal appearance tours, the Northland, as well as the Southland,

would have lost their hearts to the yodeling singer "in person," as they had already to that silvertone voice on the phonograph records and radio.

Letters from obscure, far-north Canadian villages winged their way to the Southland to tell Jimmie how the writers of those letters loved and "played over and over again" such records as "Lullaby Yodel," "I'm Lonesome Too" and "Daddy and Home."

CHAPTER THIRTY-FIVE

"Your hair has turned to silver—

"I know you're failing, too—

"Daddy, dear old Daddy—

"I'm coming home to you—."

My Jimmie certainly didn't need to toot his own horn now. The RCA Victor Company, the dealers in phonograph records, broadcasting stations, guitar manufacturers and dealers, theater owners and the reporters of theatrical news took care of all the horn-tooting business, and most efficiently, from the spring of 1928 on.

However, the theater owners, aside from the usual billing matter, had little worry about Jimmie Rodgers' publicity. His write-ups, his press notices, were legimate; not box-office.

No doubt Aaron Rodgers' youngest son had his name in some newspaper a day or so after he'd arrived on this good old earth. I know it appeared in a newspaper in Meridian when he married Rev. and Mrs. J. T. Williamson's daughter, Carrie Cecil. But I doubt very much if the name of Jimmie Rodgers appeared again "in print" until it appeared in the Asheville newspapers, in May of 1927, when it occupied a tiny portion of the few inches of space devoted to the current WWNC program.

"The Jimmy Rogers entertainers"—just like that; and in type so small that unless you were hunting for it, you'd never see it. But—were we thrilled, just the same! Even if the misspelling of both his names and the lack of an important capital "E" did make us both writhe.

But, he needed no press agent now. What he needed was an industrious press clipper. That was my joyous job. Left to his own devices I doubt if he would have made the least effort to, in this manner, preserve any record of his "meteoric rise to fame."

"Aw, shucks, Mother. That's too much work for you. Kinda nice to have 'em, maybe; but what good are they?"

But his press-books proved their value often—in more ways than one. Later they became a matter of great personal, as well as professional, pride to America's Blue Yodeler. I wish now that he had listened to me and had subscribed to a press-clipping bureau. No matter how industriously I clipped, I know there must have been many good things that I missed.

In Washington, that summer, I had to shop around for the largest "scrap book" I could find. And when I found it, they didn't have it blue! I bought just one—thinking it would never be all filled up, even with the bundles of clippings already waiting to go into it. Yet, in less than a year from that first almost-lost appearance of Jimmie's name in Asheville, that immense press-book was filled and I still had bundles of clippings. Then I found I couldn't match the first book.

Determined to have them both alike, I kept shopping—and saving the thickening bundles of clippings—until at last I found one, exactly what I wanted, in San Antonio, in May, 1933. In May!

Saving his records, one copy of each, which the Victor Company always sent us, long before they were released to the market, was in itself something of a problem sometimes. Until we built our own home. Also to be preserved was at least one copy of each photograph made of him, and the plates.

As we discovered later, we were not the only folks trying to make complete files of such things. Many fans wrote us how they were doing—or trying to do—almost the same thing! Especially, they were anxious to have a copy of every record he ever made; and a complete collection of the five song albums with their favorite's picture on the cover pages.

So, in the late summer of 1928, Jimmie was planning eagerly on going to see his old Dad. But he had first to work the string of dates Ray McCreath had booked for him. Those would take him for his first swing through his beloved Southland; his first tour of independent bookings through his old stamping ground.

A national figure now!

Down to Florida, to Miami; where once he had braked on the Florida East Coast, hurrying gaily off to work and taking with him cold, home-made biscuits in a little paper sack. To Florida, where his "bad cold," and that hollow cough had kept getting worse, so that he'd been frightened—just a little—and had decided we'd better go west, to Arizona.

To Atlanta; there to meet Ralph Peer and to sing into the mike of the portable equipment "Waiting for a Train" and his Blue Yodel Number Four—"California Blues."

Everywhere, autographing records at the Victor dealers, and broadcasting, in addition to his theater engagements; being paid handsomely, of course, for all these activities, while his royalties from records mounted steadily.

And fans wrote letters—worried, indignant letters. To us they seemed pathetically amusing.

Those fans thought everything he said—in his minstreling—was true!

They couldn't understand about Lucille, Jane, Sadie, Thelma. They sympathized with him in all his troubles—even with his gals, or when he was in jail!

They were deeply resentful toward me; indignant, because I had another "daddy" while he was in jail—or when he was a brakeman "riding the rails." They were shocked to think I could desert him; could fly to another man's arms—and even steal away his precious, golden-haired, blue-eyed baby girl!

They would have understood better, though, if they could have seen my Jimmie, in days not so long past, huddled in the middle of the bed, Turk-fashion, that big toe keeping time, those brown eyes dancing at me impudently, while he strummed and improvised those rowdy ditties about his mean mamas! And grinned, seeing our lively youngster trying to imitate him!

So—Jimmie Rodgers' answer to those friendly puzzlings was "In one-horse town or city—no matter where we are—I'm happy if I have you with me—you and my old guitar—." This—and that other sweet tribute to "his two," "Just Carrie— Anita—and me—."

But those worried, indignant letters were grand! They proved, as could nothing else, the sincerity that was in his voice as he sang.

He'd had troubles. He'd suffered. Those truths were in his songs.

He loved paying tribute to "his two" and to his old Dad.

Jimmie Rodgers' mother, Eliza Bozeman Rodgers, died while her baby boy was too young to have any but the most fleeting memories of her tender love—yet, in "Mother, the Queen of My Heart," one of his best-liked ballads, written by himself and Hoyt Bryant, there was in his voice as he sang it a haunting yearning for the mother he'd scarcely known.

But when he sang: "There's my mother—and dear old Dad—when I left I know it made them sad—so I'm going back—to that little old shack" he put quite as much feeling into his voice as though his own mother would be there to welcome him.

He had a real love for the stepmother, the present "Mother Rodgers," whom Aaron Rodgers had married late in life. And he had a great respect and deep love for the old father who'd "tried hard to bring me up right."

If Aaron Rodgers had the time of his life when his "son, Jimmie" came home that autumn of '28, so did Jimmie Rodgers, America's Blue Yodeler. It is hard to say which of them was the happier.

Jimmie's dad had a grand time showing off his boy, proudly, to the neighbors and to all his old cronies. All Geiger, Alabama, was, of course, excited and delighted. The same old Jimmie! As tickled as ever to sit hunched on somebody's back porch whanging away at a borrowed banjo, uke or mandolin.

Joyous drives to other places, where little Jimmie Rodgers had received his "smatters" of education. Scaly-bark hunts. Red and gold autumn woods. Blue skies. Folks chuckling over Jimmie's boyish pranks. "Remember that time he made himself a tent-show—and made shreds of his aunt's sheets? Said he'd buy her a dozen more old sheets. Buy all a body'd want, now, I reckon."

There were, too, folks to remind him gleefully of a certain letter written not so many months ago. "Told you I'd amount to something—someday." They knew, of course, about his getting "fired"—from WWNC—so soon after!

But nobody could say now that he hadn't made good. And nobody could be more tickled about it all than Geiger, and Scooba, and other places thereabouts.

Naturally, Jimmie was eager to do just everything for his Dad; just as he wished to share his good fortune with all his loved ones, and friends, and pals.

But Aaron Rodgers said to his boy: "Got 'bout ev'rything I want, Son. You're doin' lots for me, now—the money you send me, and all. Don't want a thing else—except, maybe, some time if you had the time, I'd kind of—like a little trip with you."

"—a little trip with you"—so he could see for himself, and enjoy, the homage that city folks everywhere were paying his son, Jimmie.

So, when Aaron Rodgers' son was playing the Keith circuit, Jimmie persuaded the old gentleman to appear with him, right out on the stage—before everybody!

I think it almost made him ill—so much excitement, such strange doin's.

His son, Jimmie, told him: "Shucks, Dad, you did just fine."

To which Aaron Rodgers protested: "Aw-w—," and chuckled.

MY HUSBAND, JIMMIE RODGERS

"I am dreaming tonight—

"Of an old Southern town—

"And the best friend that I ever had—."

CHAPTER THIRTY-SIX

"Look here, baby—you sure don't treat me very fair—
"But, baby, all of the presents you want—
"Would break a millionaire—."

And now—did Jimmie Rodgers have one grand time loading his two with gifts!

Just everything—and he did his best to pile everything on us all at one time. He kept us both just breathless. But—I knew he never could give me the one thing I most desired—a pair of good strong, healthy lungs in that frail body of his.

Excitement, the knowledge that he was right in the middle of things, of accomplishment, was keeping him up wonderfully. But, some way, I knew it couldn't last very long. So little time for real rest, complete relaxation.

Phone calls, wires, interviews. Posing for pictures. To the dressing room to make up. Perhaps a banquet, later.

But always, whenever he could manage—and he managed frequently—he would slip away between shows, and hurry to some T B hospital—there to entertain the patients.

Those visits, and his gabfests with railroad men, were to him of more importance than all the rest.

And I was learning what it meant to be the wife of a celebrity! To have around our car, whenever we drew up to the curb, a mob so dense we could scarcely squeeze through. I was learning what it meant to have interested eyes on us both, watching even every forkful of food we took in a public place. It was not long until we were obliged to resort to having nearly all of our meals sent up to our rooms.

Not that we didn't, both of us, appreciate the warm friendliness for a well-loved star that lay deep in those interested eyes. I know. In other days I had been just as eager to "see him"—or her—and his family, too! Jimmie and I would certainly have stared plenty at Anita Stewart, that time in New Orleans—if we'd had the chance.

But a sick boy can't rest very well, can't relax, when he knows strange eyes, however friendly and admiring, are on his every movement, even during his un-public hours. The time came—when he was scarcely able to work at all; when the effort of getting to the theater, getting made up and doing his act was almost too much for him that he would say wearily:

"Let's get a cottage at a tourist court, next town. More privacy. Quieter. Sometimes I can hardly stand the confusion, the constant movement, in hotels. You don't mind, do you, Mother?"

Mind! When a tiny furnished cabin was about the only homey home we could have. And I could fix for him the cornbread-and-milk he loved. And have for him his good old cane syrup.

I have been asked frequently why it was that with his wasting-away lungs, and the importance of caring for his voice, Jimmie persisted in smoking cigarettes so incessantly. There was really nothing so surprising about it. When you stop to consider, there were very few pleasures which he was able to enjoy, and of those, smoking was one of his greatest. To Jimmie there was no such thing as a bad cigarette. The only distinction he drew was that some were better than others. From late boyhood, I believe, he had smoked every brand, to say nothing of the many occasions when, for sake of economy, he had been obliged to roll his own. However, because of the necessity for avoiding irritation as much as possible, without being obliged to cut down the amount of his smoking, the time did arrive when he gave very careful thought to the selection of a brand that would become his "permanent smoke." I am not sure just what experiments he tried, nor by what steps he finally reached his decision, but I do know that for several years one of my jobs was to see that he was kept always and plentifully supplied with Old Golds.

He was as stubborn as ever about that "give-up" business, though. I've known him to work with a temperature so high he scarcely knew what was going on or where he was. "No, now, Mother—I'm all right. Those folks, lots of 'em, have come from long ways off to see me. I ain't goin' to disappoint 'em."

They came—from long ways off, lots of them. There was no doubt, those days, even in his own mind, about being "ovationed." Show-wise city people in great theaters on the Loew, the Keith-Orpheum, the Interstate, ovationed him. Humble, smalltown country folk ovationed him when he could no longer manage four shows a day on the major circuits and was appearing with tent shows or playing wildcat dates in out of the way villages because, that way, he need give only one brief performance daily, and could still feel that he was "useful"—not yet ready to sit in the sun, with folded hands, for days on end.

Folks came; many of them with gifts. Fine pipes. Fine dogs. Things men like to give men. Gifts from sweet-faced country mothers—things mothers like to give idolized sons. Those humble little country gifts pleased and touched Jimmie Rodgers, minstrel, more than all the finer gifts.

Down at Beeville, Texas, a cotton-farmer's wife waited after "the show" to make her way back to his dressing room. No doubt she was inwardly much disturbed by her unwonted daring, being unused to backstage regions. Sturdily, if timidly, she made her way to him, in her hands a pasteboard box—a shoe box.

She looked at my Jimmie—something like adoration in her eyes. She fairly thrust the box at him, with a choking little: "For—you."

That was all. She was gone.

Jimmie and I, both, had to cry a little—over that little box. Just some flowers;

some little home-grown country chrysanthemums. Sweeter, finer, richer than all the flowers in the world—to Jimmie Rodgers. And—to me.

In one large city theater the SRO sign had been taken down; the box office closed; no more tickets could possibly be sold. A man approached one of the door guards belligerently. He declared bluntly: "I've come to see Jimmie Rodgers—and I'm going to see him! So you might as well let me in!"

There was some commotion about it—but he saw Jimmie Rodgers.

In a small town in Tennessee an old mountaineer couple, the woman quiet and meek; the man grim-faced, lanky, pushed their way to the ticket window the moment the doors were opened. The old fellow informed:

"We-uns driv over hunnerd mile, horse an' buggy, jist to git to see this boy. We-uns ain't got nary cent. But—we-uns is comin' in—Mandy an' me!"

Mandy an' me went in.

Perhaps, once on a time not so very long ago, a shy young fellow with a wistful smile and a hacking little cough, wearing a smeared mask of burnt cork, had plinked his banjo near the general store in their crossroads mountain village.

Perhaps "Mandy an' me" remembered the sweet southern voice and the tender little story about Sammie and Nettie, they played on their talking machine, or heard some neighbor play.

Asheville? Yes, there, too, Jimmie went. And "the gang"; the railroad men, the local musicians, Fred Jones and the rest of the police were jubilant. "Same old Jimmie! Big-headed? I should say not!"

No—Jimmie Rodgers never thought himself too good for anybody. "The underest dog is just as good as I am—and I'm just as good as the toppest dog." Never, to the last, did he change his mind about that.

He held no rancor against those who had failed to appreciate his humble efforts in days past. Perhaps, as he told me, it wasn't that they didn't like him. Sometimes "office politics" interfere with a man's career.

Gladly, with simple friendliness, Jimmie responded now to a request to broadcast—over WWNC.

Asheville; where once we'd had such "daggone tough sleddin'." Where he'd played nursemaid to a furnace in exchange for shelter for himself and his two.

And Wickes Wamboldt, beloved columnist of the Carolinas, devoted his syndicated column, one day, entirely to the Victor Recording Star. He told of having heard Jimmie when he was an unknown making his first broadcast.

"He was singing a lullaby. His voice had a peculiar, haunting, sympathetic, descriptive character. I could see him rocking the baby, crooning over it tenderly."

The columnist went on to tell how then he'd phoned the station, inquiring who this fellow was. "He isn't anybody; just a bum." He told then of his talk over the phone with the boy himself, who was broke, disheartened, having been removed from the program; and of how he'd then phoned the station again in Jimmie's behalf. "They answered me guardedly. The management apparently did not share my interest in Jimmie Rodgers' talent—Jimmie Rodgers' fairy-like good fortune is due to something that was born in him if he had not plugged along it would not have been brought out. But if the gift of the gods had not been in him, all his plugging would not have done any more for him, perhaps, than make him a good railroad hand."

When I read that my mind went back to that day my heartsick boy had been trying to compose two letters; one to the Brunswick people—and one to the Victor Company; and had been called to the phone—.

Of all the fine, tender little stories that have been written about Jimmie Rodgers, somehow I treasure this story of Wickes Wamboldt's the most.

MY HUSBAND, JIMMIE RODGERS

"Goin' down the road—feelin' bad—

"But I ain't goin' to be treated that way—

"Yodel-ay-ee-o-lee-o-ee-ee—."

CHAPTER THIRTY-SEVEN

"And I can't be bothered—

"With all these old hard times—."

New Orleans. Keith's Orpheum. Jimmie Rodgers, headliner. Hotelling at the Jung. Drawing down a thousand a week as a vaudeville star. "Averaging one hundred thousand yearly from his Victor records." "His reception an ovation"—"plays guitar as though had grown up with one on his lap"—"May be classed as an Orleanian."—"Known to millions."

New Orleans; where he once amused himself and others with a cheap guitar, and sang in a quaint little way that was all his own.

New Orleans, city of memories for us; my Jimmie's name in lights where once, on that runaway three-day honeymoon of ours, we had sat and stared wide-eyed at our favorite, Anita Stewart.

And what other memories the city contained for us! Tender, poignant, very vivid. The years had really been few.

There was that time, a few months after our marriage, when my young brakeman husband actually had a job; braking a worktrain. We had to live in a cheap railroad boarding house at a lonely junction. Nothing tasted good to the young girl wife of Jimmie Rodgers. She craved fresh fruit. The little general store had nothing but insipid, tasteless oranges.

"Look, Sweetheart. See what I got for you." Out of a pocket of his blue overalls Jimmie fished a double handful of ripe, sweet plums. "Swiped 'em, Sugar," he told me grinning.

"Jimmie! You—stole them?"

"Yep. Out of a pail sittin' right out on the porch of the post office where somebody'd left 'em for me. Wasn't a soul lookin'. Made up my mind my wife was goin' to have that fresh fruit she's been honin' for. So—I just helped myself—and came along. You need 'em, Honey. They're good. I tried one—just to see if they'd be all right for you."

Good? Not if they were—stolen! But—they were!

That wasn't all, though. His run took him to New Orleans, forty miles away. But the yards were far from fruit stands, and he had little time to shop. But once he caught a butch on a delayed passenger, and shelled out a whole dime for one peach. It was a gorgeous thing, crimson and gold.

"Gosh, Sugar—like to never got it safe home to you without squashing it. Go on and eat it, why don't you?"

It was just too gorgeous to eat. And I was—crying, with that beautiful peach in my two hands, turning it over and over—just looking at it; thinking that no matter how sweet it might taste, it could be no sweeter than my beloved brakie—always surprising me in delightful, unselfish little ways.

New Orleans. Once, not long ago, jobless, broke, discouraged—almost—he had trudged Canal Street, shoes full of holes, stomach empty, thin body racked by a hacking little cough. Christmas season, and not a penny to buy little presents for his wife and two babies in Meridian. Then, hopping a freight for Meridian—while a messenger with a death message was searching New Orleans for an unknown transient named Jimmie Rodgers.

And—New Orleans, where Jimmie Rodgers had bought my engagement ring! A whole year, I think, after we had been married. I suppose once more Jimmie's watch and chain had gone to see uncle. It went—many times; but never, that I can remember, for anything for himself.

I do remember well that time it went to see uncle in Meridian, when our second baby, June Rebecca, arrived. The overjoyed young father thanked "doctor" all over the lot. And went scurrying to town—to uncle—as fast as he could go! Came back—with twenty-five dollars. Grinned to "doctor": "All I could rake up this time, Doc. But I'll sure get you some more, right quick. Gosh, I sure thank you."

In fact, my husband thanked the doctor so much, so often, so fervently, that I finally complained to Mother: "You'd almost think nobody had anything to do with her getting here—except the doctor!"

Meridian. Memories piled on memories. If any of our home town folks suspected that Jimmie Rodgers, Exclusive Victor Recording Star—and all the rest of it— would come back to strut around and razz all who'd predicted he'd "come to no good," they found they were mistaken. He was the same as always—and there had been few, if any, I believe, who had even feared otherwise.

Oldtimers and newtimers, alike, clasped his hand, assuring him of their genuine pride in his success. And Jimmie Rodgers was prouder of those sincere handclasps than of all his success.

And the kids! Jimmie Rodgers had been known to all of them—all their lives. But that had been the old Jimmie Rodgers—not this glamorous world-figure who had come among them now.

My parents' home in Meridian was near a schoolhouse, and the kids felt they just must see Jimmie before taking up their work for the day. So they came to the house—before Jimmie was out of bed. But what of that? Into the house they filed, and through the bedroom, in a long line, shaking hands with and grinning shyly at this other boy, who grinned back at them from the bed.

As the last of that long line filed out through the door, Jimmie looked at me and laughed: "Gosh, Mother. I feel like a new baby the neighbors all had to come and see."

On that, our first trip back home, Jimmie and I both felt a childish satisfaction in driving through the streets of Meridian in our beloved blue Buick—even though it was, by then, a few months old. The streets were full of much finer cars, of course, but it had been here in Meridian that we had lingered in front of a plate glass window, wishing we could have even just one ride in one of those pretty new Buicks, and where Jimmie insisted stoutly: "I'm goin' to get you one, Sugar—some day."

And—that long-fought-for security? Well—why worry now? We had it, didn't we? Or did we? Anyway, those Victor records of his were something tangible. They were our security. No matter what happened now—they'd continue on—and on—and on—.

"Money's no good until after it's spent—."

So, utterly foolish, like two kids who'd never expected to see so grand a Christmas tree, we spent our money, right and left! Expenses? Who cares? Just a word, anyway. But—we didn't spend it all on ourselves, by any means.

Jimmie Rodgers was a boy who wanted everybody—hobos and all—to share his Christmas tree.

Even when, because of his "position," some unscrupulous merchant would take advantage and cunningly tip the bill, sometimes double, Jimmie would pay—with never a protest. But he'd grin to me: "Shucks, Mother—the poor devil's just fightin' to keep out of the red, maybe."

On the other hand, so many splendid gifts were piled on him—even by merchants. And managers of fine hotels would wire us, when they heard we were to be in their city, inviting us to be their guests.

So now we found ourselves with "possessions." What to do? We were running the Williamson family out of house and home, storing our stuff. Besides, our daughter, within a few years—would be a young lady!

MY HUSBAND, JIMMIE RODGERS

"Gosh, Mother. Looks like we'd better be thinkin' about gettin' ourselves a home somewhere."

A home! Well, I loved housekeeping; loved a pretty kitchen and the joy of preparing tempting food for my boy. A home! Where the three of us could be—so happy together.

We'd get a home in Meridian. Be near the folks. But—no. I knew that moist Delta climate, that low altitude, would be bad for those wasting lungs.

Washington? Decidedly not—much as we both loved the Capital City. Winters there were too cold. My darling could never live through another such winter as we'd spent there.

Arizona? No-o—. California? Perhaps.

But—it made Jimmie no never mind. He just grabbed his old guitar, grinned at me, and sang:

"I'm goin' to build me a shanty—Lord! I'm goin' to settle down—get me a corn-fed mama—Lord! And quit runnin' 'round—."

CHAPTER THIRTY-EIGHT

"Where the whip-poor-wills—

"Sing me to sleep at night—

"And the eagle roosts—

"On rocks of the mountain—."

Gypsyfootin'. "All around we'll wander—first we're here and then we're there." In very truth, now. But with a definite purpose.

No need now for that old gay command: "Throw your things together, kid." Our traveling things were always together—in orderly arrangement, months on end. We knew weeks, often months, ahead of time just which "here" we'd be leaving for which "there."

But it couldn't be: "Here we go, just we three—." It was so summers, sometimes, when we could have our Nita with us. We were content—but too busy, most of the time, for our old, gay, teasing companionship. I sort of longed, sometimes, to hear my Jimmie say again: "I'll get it for you some time, Sugar. I'll make good."

He'd made good. There was nothing—except strong, healthy lungs for himself—which I could possibly wish for, that my husband could not provide for me "at the drop of a hat."

He was a man of affairs these days. Just the same, we managed, now and then, little runaway vacations. Sometimes just the two of us. But whenever possible, Jimmie would say: "Just think, Mother. Goin' to have a week's lay-off, then me and my two will go places."

And then my boy would be his old carefree, happy-hearted self; teasing his two; racing trains to astonish the "hoghead, swellhead, two empty head and a baked head" with his "thumbs up" signal; pretending to pull a bellcord, and giving them his now famous "whoo-whoo-oo-oo—."

Sometimes when we traveled by train Jimmie would disappear. I'd learn later that he'd crawled into the cab with the engineer—to help speed the limited over the silver rails. "Gosh, mother. That sure was fun!"

So, on one of those vacations we headed for Texas–"a place I surely love."

And I said to Jimmie: "Darling, this is the place for you! Let's—settle down 'where the sunshine spends the winter.' It isn't too far from Meridian. I like it here—and you've always loved Texas. Let's."

Jimmie considered that. But he demurred: "Kind of out of the way, though for my business. Okay, Sugar. We'll look around, maybe. You're the boss. What you say goes."

But—Texas is so darn big! It has so many different kinds of climate—and so many different altitudes. I knew he'd need dry air, warm winters, a fairly high altitude. I learned that all those could be found in "The Heart o' the Hills" in Kerrville, South Texas. In fact, one of the government hospitals for tubercular service men is located there: Legion.

Anyway, we'd give it a look-see. We'd rent a furnished cottage and spend the rest of our vacation there. But easier said than done! Not a cottage to be had, it seemed. All rented—to wives of patients out at Legion. Still—there was a "private home," the owner away, but—no, the guardian couldn't rent it out—to tourists.

But when he learned who wanted it—the place was ours!

And that very night came a long distance call for Jimmie. We had no phone, of course—but the operator asked our next-door neighbor to "please call Jimmie Rodgers."

As it happened, our next door neighbor, all unknowing, was at that very moment reading a story in a San Antonio newspaper which told of the brief visit of the Victor star and vaudeville headliner to Texas. She had just remarked to her husband: "O—Jimmie Rodgers is in Texas. My—how I wish we could see him."

Then, gasping into the telephone: "Jimmie Rodgers! Not—not the famous blue yodeler!"

And Mrs. W. B. Powell, of Kerrville, now one of my closest friends, has often told me how she nearly fainted with surprise and excitement before she could find breath to tell her husband the news.

Then—we bought ourselves some Texas soil—in Westland Hills, Kerrville. Now—exciting times planning Jimmie's "shanty." When that fifty-thousand dollar home was completed, to the last drape, my ex-brakie was a pretty proud young husband.

"Mother—know what? If you don't mind, I'd—sorta like to call it—Blue Yodeler's Paradise. Think that'd be okay?"

I told him then: "This home is yours, darling. And do you remember the caption one of the San Antonio newspapers ran over the picture of this house in the Sunday section?"

Jimmie grinned and nodded: "Yep, 'the home that yodels built.' But I thought maybe you—look, Sugar, I don't give a doggone what anybody else might say or think. It's just that I thought—hoped—maybe you'd like it: Blue Yodeler's Paradise."

"Of course, Jimmie. I do like it."

So—the blue yodels, born on the wind-scoured plains of Texas, came back—home to live 'mid Texas bluebonnets—away out on the mountain.

But—Jimmie wasn't satisfied. He didn't feel, some way, that he'd done enough for me. He felt there surely must be something else he could do. He couldn't rest until he was convinced I had just everything to make me perfectly happy.

He told me, near tears: "Carrie, you stuck by me—through everything. And never a complaint. In my railroadin' days, you would get up out of a sound sleep to fix me some breakfast—smilin', whether I was just leavin' for a run, or just comin' in, all tired and hungry and cold. You've gone hungry and cold. You've worried—O, I know. But, you stuck—kept cheerful. Now I just can't seem to figure out how I can best make it all up to you. What else can I get for you, Sweetheart? Isn't there—something?"

"Nothing in the world, Darling. You've given me—everything. But—I haven't kept my promise to you!" He looked so puzzled I hurried on: "You know, Jimmie, I've promised you—over and over—to let my hair grow out again."

He grinned at that; thought a moment, then told me earnestly: "Gosh, Sugar. I sure wish you would. I—I like women to look like women. I mean-aw, shucks, you know what I mean—."

"Of course. Well, I'm going to let it grow now—sure enough—maybe." I'd learned to add that "maybe" to all promises about that hair-growing business. I'd been wearing my hair in a long bob, but every time it started to really get long I would become so annoyed with it I'd have it whacked off again.

When we were first married, my young brakie had never had much to say about my hair even though it was so long and thick. We never discussed my bobbing it. I just took a sudden notion one day, and Sister Annie had chopped it off for me. Well, I didn't know, until then, how much Jimmie had liked my long hair. From then on he didn't let me forget it, though. So—for some six years I'd been making solemn promises—with reservations.

Jimmie was leaving for a short tour—leaving me behind this time—but I knew he'd come back home for Christmas, if he had to come by plane. Our first Christmas in our new home—the only home of any kind we'd ever owned. We'd have a grand Christmas. All our previous Christmases had been so pitifully bleak. For our little Nita's sake, as well as our own, Blue Yodeler's Paradise should be joyous with Yuletide cheer.

Blue Yodeler's Paradise, neither then nor ever, knew anything of formality. You came and were heartily welcomed; you did as you pleased, stayed as long as you could and went away when you wished—with the native Texan's "hurry back" ringing in your ears.

Sometimes its young master would be there to welcome you; sometimes not. If there, he might be lively, full of happy-hearted laughter, little-boy mischief, or he might be writhing in pain; a specialist there, a trained nurse, his fine open-doored home hushed and terrified.

Even the beautiful Heart o' the Hills country can do nothing for a boy with lung-trouble—if he insists he isn't ready to be dubbed a "has-been"; if he refuses to "give up." If the restless feet, the eager, singing Irish heart of him, resist deserting the grand hustle-bustle that is Life.

There could be—and were—others with him now, when on the road, to relieve him of all the bothersome little details of everyday living; to take his phone calls, keep his books, look after his mail. Even to relieve him of the small effort of opening doors and of lifting the case containing that famous old guitar. His strength must be saved—so another weakening spasm of coughing might be delayed; so he could meet people, step out on the stage, smile wistfully and croon softly or yodel gaily.

Did any smile at the ex-brakie and his retinue—chauffeur, secretary, booking manager? If so, it made him no never mind—nor me. But I don't really think they did. They realized he was only a shell of a man; a precious shell-fighting as bravely, as unwhimperingly, now against his old enemy, that old T B, as he'd fought disappointments, heartbreak and sickness through all the years—still smilin' through.

At home or away Jimmie had a lovable little-boy delight in surprises. I don't mean for himself; though he enjoyed them, too. But he'd go to great lengths, sometimes—puzzling hard just to have the pleasure of surprising me—of seeing my eyes widen with joy, of watching my little gasp of delight.

When he was away scarcely a day passed without some little surprise gift; if nothing more than a box of candy. And he always managed in some way to make it surprising—to add a bit of mystery or novelty. No matter where he was, in what exciting activities, with what gay companions or however exhausted, he was always giving thought—taking a bit of extra time and energy—to send something that had always a unique personal touch; especially for his two.

That desolate December day when we'd clung together, back in 1923, beside our little dark-eyed June Rebecca's newly-made grave, my husband had told me, shockingly: "Never, never again, will I fail to let you know, some way, Sweetheart, where or how to reach me. If I'm ever away from you again you'll hear from me, some way, every single day." He kept that solemn promise to the letter.

Then—as the 1929 Yuletide season approached I patted myself on the back. My hair was actually long enough to be rolled into a little bun. How pleased Jimmie would be! He'd be home for Christmas. Just try to keep him away! Our first Christmas, the three of us together, in our own home!

Meet him at the Sunset Station, in San Antonio. The very same station where I'd had my first glimpse of the Alma City, that time we'd crawled off the eastbound from Tucson, a tired, shabby, broke but happy three; homeless, jobless. We'd spend the night there, and drive home to the hills in the morning.

But when I arrived Jimmie Rodgers was already there—at the Gunter. It was late. We had so much to talk about. Go eat; talk while eating.

Happy, excited, looking so well, he gave me not even time to take off my hat. And I was so anxious to hear what he'd say—about my hair! Of course, under my tight-fitting turban, he couldn't see my little bun.

But he seemed so rushed, so insistent. Just barely did he give me a breath's time to dab some powder at my nose. Then to the elevator. To the street.

"Where are we going? I thought we were going to eat?" My proud young husband marched me to the curb. A car was there; a beautiful long-hooded, shining new

Packard. Well—what of it? Plenty of expensive limousines on Houston Street, in San Antonio, any hour of any day.

Jimmie opened the door of that gorgeous car, and commanded me: "Get in. Just want you to sit in it a minute. See what you think of it."

"But, Jimmie! The owner might—."

"Aw, shucks, Mother, just see how it sits."

Well—it "sat" all right. Lovely, of course—but I was hungry. What about eating?

Still excited, my husband fairly raced me back up to our rooms—and put into my hands some papers with my name on them.

I, Carrie Cecil Williamson Rodgers, was the owner of that grand seven-passenger Packard!

Always I had to cry—not merely from joy; from pride in and gratitude to Jimmie Rodgers, the section foreman's little boy.

Jimmie comforted me, and fumbled that turban off my head, so I could cry better. And—discovered my little bun!

Well—he was so happy—over a little thing like that—I couldn't help remembering the time he'd thanked the doctor all over the lot for bringing us our little June.

Immediately he urged me to "fix" my face, so we could go eat. But once more he wanted me to go to the car and see how it "sat." And—suddenly—he left me there; still hungry, but still winking back some tears—and so happy.

He was there again—shoving a little package into my hands. I sat staring—at a diamond brooch!

"Aw, shucks, Mother. Now don't you go to bawlin' again. That's—daggone it— that's just 'cause I like your hair that way."

At long last, when we finally were at table, from the radio came:

"No money in my pocket—I'm loafin' 'round so flat—I'll think of you, mean mama—."

CHAPTER THIRTY-NINE

"Though we may have quarreled—
"Please don't say good bye—."

And—now! Was Jimmie Rodgers always sunny-natured? Could he—always—take just everything, the good and the bad, with the same sweet, patient smile? Didn't he have even one tiny little spark of fire—of temper?

Well, Jimmie Rodgers was Irish. What do you think?

After that runaway three-day honeymoon of ours, when Jimmie Rodgers, rail-roader, and his schoolgirl bride went back—not ashamed or regretful, but a bit uncertain, maybe—home to Meridian for the parental blessing, it was my old Dad who gave us some good advice.

It was brief, in words he had used on many other similar occasions—and which had been used from time immemorial by other understanding ministers, who knew and loved their flocks.

Said Dad gravely, while his eyes twinkled: "Remember, children; whatever you do, wherever you go, always take the two bears along with you; bear and forbear."

But we had been too busy laughing together—or comforting each other—through the ensuing years to give much thought to a couple of bears. They had been—some-how—those two bears—very easy to manage. It isn't much use—or satisfaction—to keep up a one-sided fuss. When the fussee just grins at, or kisses, the fussor, the fuss just naturally sighs, and gives up.

But—yes—my Jimmie could blow up quite royally on occasion.

His temper was like a vivid flash of lightning. It came suddenly; then was gone, and the sun shone again. Never did he indulge in any sulking. If his outburst had resulted in hurt feelings to somebody, he was instantly contrite.

But—prolonged, intense physical suffering can sometimes nick the sunniest soul. It was only during the last year or so—and then not often—that he might unthinkingly give me a short answer. Yet, no matter how sick or in what agony he might be, he would say instantly, regardless of whether we were alone or with others: "O, Carrie—I oughtn't to have said that, that way. I just don't know what made me."

But when Jimmie Rodgers gave way to a real display of temper it was never because of any wrong toward himself; but for some wrong, real or fancied, toward somebody or something he loved.

One of those boyish outbursts occurred when we were living in Kerrville. In fact, it was quite the most explosive exhibition of temper I'd ever encountered—from that sunny-hearted Irishman! It was laughable—even though most difficult to cope with at the time. To express it mildly, he was pretty mad.

The young master of Blue Yodeler's Paradise had been away several days, but would be home today. He had not been any too well when he left, and I couldn't help worrying, although he assured me each day, by long distance: "Now, now Mother, don't you worry. I'm all right."

Still, his voice didn't sound quite as cheery as usual. It sounded tired.

On the day he was coming I'd ordered fresh fruit—white and blue grapes, pears, tangerines; and some fine big apples for their splash of color. He'd nibble at the grapes, perhaps. That would be all, but just the sight of a basket of fruit beside his bed pleased him.

Too, I refilled his atomizer with the new, exotic perfume he said he liked. Refilled his cigarette box with his favorite Old Golds. Laid out a flannel robe, flannelette pajamas, comfortable slippers—so he could be made comfortable immediately without waiting for his bag to be unpacked.

In the kitchen Anna, my colored girl, was busily preparing his cornbread. Although we knew from experience that was probably all he would eat—cornbread and milk—we'd planned, just the same, to have a juicy planked sirloin, with many other things. Contentedly busy, Anna was crooning one of her own little croons. The daughter of the house, Miss Anita Rodgers, wouldn't be home from school for a couple of hours yet.

It was winter time; real winter and below zero in the northern states, but true to custom, the sunshine had been spending the winter in South Texas.

Then, to the Heart o' the Hills, to Kerrville, came one of the Lone Star State's famed northers to hit suddenly, without a breath of warning. No doubt the radio had warned, but I'd been too busy to listen. A norther—a white norther, at that; most unusual for South Texas. When we had snow, that was an event.

The thermometer tumbled rapidly to near freezing. Skies leadened. Then slowly, but surely, a white film covered the street, the walks, the lawn. I wasn't worried about Jimmie. He had everything in the car to make him warm, dry and comfortable. Somebody would bring Nita home in a closed car.

But—I heard the protesting whine of a dog. Then another—and others. Calling Anna, I hurried to a storage closet; snatched armfuls of old sweaters, blankets, car robes—and, shivering, the two of us raced to the kennels where the young master's half-dozen or more pets—gifts from admirers—were yelping, whining and trembling in the sudden cold.

It was no use.

Anna exclaimed: "Can y'magine it!"

Nothing we could do about it. Any minute the car would be turning in. My darling would be disappointed if I failed to welcome him home properly. Still shivering, teeth chattering, we raced for the house—and heard the siren. Jimmie Rodgers was home again.

But he looked so pitiful; his features gray and drawn, though not with cold. He insisted: "Sure, I'm all right, Sugar. Just—a little tired. Guess I'll get to bed pretty quick." He turned then to tell the chauffeur: "You can go bring our girl home."

The chauffeur was bringing Jimmie's bag and guitar in. I ran to find Nita's sweater and her leather coat. When I came back Jimmie had disappeared. Well, he'd gone on to bed. But—he wasn't up there. Where? Again I heard the dogs protesting; and hurried to the kitchen phone. I'd order straw or something.

I said to Anna: "Where'd Jimmie go? Have you seen him?"

"Yes'm. He came out; say hello to me."

"Well—I can't find him. Where'd he disappear to?"

"He gone to the dogs."

"Wh-what?"

"I mean—he gone see how is they gettin' 'long. Is they f'eezin'."

There was repressed glee on Anna's good brown face; glee mingled oddly with apprehension. "I tried t'tell him. Jes wouldn't lissen. He find out! He ain't f'm Mississippi; he f'm Missouri!"

As I raced out the back, heading for the kennels, I heard distress in our Anna's soft negro voice as she called: "He goin' die-an'-catch noomonia—sure nuff."

I fairly collided with a furious Jimmie Rodgers. He passed me as if I were not in existence. Fury made him strong. He stamped into the house; through the house. I followed, doing my best to explain. Fury had closed his ears, but had loosed his tongue.

I was a heathen. The servants were heathens. Anybody in the whole damn world that would neglect poor helpless creatures, just leave 'em to freeze to death—was a heathen. He heard not one word I was saying. Straight to the big linen closet he marched. Snatched an armful of the first wool objects his hands touched; two pairs of beautiful, soft, white wool blankets! And still he would not listen.

Out to the kennels, still berating a cold, cruel world—and everybody in it. Pink tongues daily over-reached themselves trying to kiss him, his cheeks, his hands. Dogs large, dogs small, whimpered and yipped their greetings to their adoring and adored master. Chains rattled.

At the fourth kennel he was out of material. He stood up, brushed the snow from his trousers knees and overcoat—and—stared.

Presently, he said, to nobody in particular: "Well—I'll be dogged!"

It was a most shamed, most contrite young husband who trudged back through that thin carpet of snow toward the house, and in—to the warmth and fragrance of Anna's immaculate kitchen—there to drink gratefully a steaming cup of rich coffee, thick with cream.

I had no need to say: "I told you so!" Nor even to remind him that I'd tried to tell him—that just as fast as Anna and I had poked warm coverings into their kennels, just that fast his pets had pulled and dragged everything out again, tearing it to shreds.

So—he was ashamed, and not ashamed of being ashamed.

That night he came back downstairs, in robe and pajamas, to sit for a little while with his two before the fireplace. And when Nita brought his guitar to him, and begged him to sing for her, he rounded his eyes, pretending great surprise and told her: "Why, Baybo—we got a whole basement full of my singin'."

But our daughter informed him: "I don't care, Daddy! I'd rather hear you, your-self, sing to me. Not old phonograph records."

She cuddled at his knees while he strummed gently and crooned; and winked at me over her small head. She looked up indignantly when I laughed. But, how could I help it?

"Got me a pretty mama—got me a bulldog, too—My mama—she don't love me—but my poor bulldog, he do—."

CHAPTER FORTY

"Where a man is a man—

"And a friend is a friend—

"Where all my cares and worries end—."

In spite of Jimmie's emotional outburst—or maybe because of it—he rested better than usual that night. When he discovered the morning sun he insisted on coming down to Anna's kitchen for his grapefruit and coffee. But he'd forgotten his cigarettes. I told Anna: "I'll bring some from the living room. And maybe you can persuade him to eat a hot biscuit."

Some mail. Quite a lot, as usual. I sorted out Jimmie's, got a pack of Old Golds, and hurried back to the kitchen.

Jimmie was enjoying his dunking; hot biscuit in cane syrup. Besides his pajamas, flannel robe and slippers, he was wearing a sort of shamed little grin. Anna was chuckling.

She was saying: "I done heerd you say, Mistah Jimmie, jest lotsa times—I jes natchally likes the best an' I b'lieve in takin' it.'—Heh, heh. You-all sho didn't skip it."

Jimmie sipped his coffee, blew a puff of smoke at her and said: "Yeah, daggone it—but if I'd known anything like that was goin' to happen—well, I'd have made you a present of 'em, maybe. But—only thing is—there's poor devils half freezin' to death in some of those little hid-out shacks down along the Guadalupe. Mother, you and me'll go see what we can do for 'em—today, sometime. I owe it to 'em

MY HUSBAND, JIMMIE RODGERS

—for blowin' up that way."

"All right, darling, but remember you'll have to blue-yodel a couple of times extra, at your next recording, to pay for those brand-new, all wool—."

Jimmie just grinned: "Aw-w—," and busied himself with his letters.

Business letters. More offers—which were, in fact, urgent requests to "come here," "go there"; personal appearance tours. Independent dates, major circuit tours; northern states, Canada. Mexico wanted him. England wanted him. South America wanted him.

Fan letters. Just a word or two in your own handwriting, Jimmie. A little picture of any kind; a snapshot will do. Be so happy, and proud. We do hope you'll come out our way, some time; near enough so we can get to see you. You have such a beautiful way of sending your songs right to one's heart. With your records we are not so lonesome. Cheerful. Gay. Touching. Heaven bless you, Jimmie—and keep your beautiful voice strong and clear and your heart light—.

His secretary came. The thin carpet of snow that had come with leaden skies had long gone. Texas skies were blue again. Beyond the lawn, velvety green and shining, a party of tourists had parked their car—to kodak the brick-and-tile home of Jimmie Rodgers, America's Blue Yodeler.

When his secretary had gone, my husband told me: "I'd kind of planned on making those northern and foreign tours. Be kind of nice. But—takes me too far away from Texas. You and Baybo'd go with me, of course—but—some way I'd just sort of rather—well, go to the woods. You know what I mean."

I knew. He had received one offer—"forty-one straight weeks at eighteen hundred dollars per week"—but he was looking at a fan letter in his hands.

Just a couple of sheets of cheap tablet paper, the letter written in pencil. Some of his letters, many of them, were written in ink, and on very correct stationery—but however written, the messages were, in effect, the same.

MY HUSBAND, JIMMIE RODGERS

And I remembered a phrase from one of his many write-ups: "Jimmie Rodgers charms others as he has already captured the hearts of simple folk whose songs he sings."

His friend and recording manager, Ralph Peer, had wired him: "Watch your health carefully, as it is worth more than ten thousand per."

Jimmie Rodgers would, I knew, accept the more lucrative engagements—if he chose; regardless of any advice doctors—or I—might give him.

But he continued regarding that humble letter, thoughtfully. Presently he passed it over to me.

"—we read where you sometimes visit the small towns—come to our section? Make us so happy. Cities too far away for us to get there—. We pray to have the pleasure of really seeing our favorite radio and phonograph star—."

I remembered then something he'd said to me, a few years back: "If I had money so's I could afford it, I think I'd like nothing better'n just troupin' with tent shows— all the time."

Jimmie's earnings had been, and were, high. They would, no doubt, continue so, for some time, at least, even if he did nothing more, ever, but sit in the sun with folded hands. Yet—money rolled away from us as fast as it sped toward us; and would keep on doing that, I knew. In his railroading days, whenever he had a stake I helped him spend his money, gaily; because he wanted me to—and because I en- joyed it. Now—it was just the same.

At least, it may be said of us that we kept cash in circulation—much of it—in Texas all through the Great Depression.

If either of us saw something we longed to possess, we bought it—without a second thought. We made loans, too, casually and without security—lifting friends and mere acquaintances out of tight spots. My boy's hospital, nurse and doctor bills were becoming increasingly heavy.

MY HUSBAND, JIMMIE RODGERS

So-all the money Jimmie Rodgers could possibly bring in would, it seemed, never be enough. Now, with these attractive offers—what?

My Jimmie took the humble little letter as I passed it back to him, without comment. He looked up at me and said: "We've been spending an awful lot of money, haven't we." I nodded. It was a statement, not a question.

He laid the letter on the low table by his side, lighted an Old Gold, glanced again at the cheap tablet-paper pages, and asked: "All right, Mother?"

I told him, smiling: "I was hoping you would."

He was pleased and relieved. "Gosh, that's that!"

Then he added worriedly: "Means showin' at cheap prices. Won't make a fourth as much money. Means bein' at my own expense more. And it means—cheapenin' myself professionally.

"But I don't give a daggone! They're my folks. When it comes right down to it, I get more kick out of knowin' I've—well, you know—."

I knew. "—cities too far for us to get there—make us so happy—." These fan letters—these personal appeals; almost prayers. Because of them and because of the more leisurely life, my husband, Jimmie Rodgers, vaudeville headliner, radio star, Exclusive Victor Recording Artist, would "go to the woods."

The man who could fill any theater in any city at any time, would appear in village schoolhouses, town halls and even in tents. His own people had called—and he could respond.

And I was glad. He could still be, in some measure, in the grand hustle-bustle that was Life—as he had to be or consider himself "out of it all." At the same time, his work would be so much less exhausting. Short, leisurely drives from one "spot" to the next. One ten-minute performance instead of four-a-day. Folks. Lots of folks. His kind of folks. He could loaf around the lot; talk shop with folks who talked his language, play with the dogs and kids; be gay. And he could watch the old smokies headin' in. Give 'em thumbs up, grinning—wistfully.

"Yes, Jimmie. I'll go with you, of course."

So today, in obscure little villages in many parts of the South there are Jimmie Rodgers fans who treasure "tonighters," usually printed on plain news stock, which announce "Added Attraction Extraordinary"—"World Famous Singer—Jimmie Rodgers in person."

Much of the type was handset, some of the letters upside-down, and the cuts, showing Jimmie with his old guitar, were smutched and spotted with ink smears, making him look as though he were peering out through a black snowstorm.

But how those tonighters did draw! How the country folks—his own folks—did flock in and crowd tent or town hall, good-naturedly edging closer together so one—or a dozen—more eager neighbors could crowd in and see and hear too.

Cheapen him professionally? Nothing could do that. And if it had, who cared? Not Jimmie Rodgers, minstrel. He had come home!

Of all that experience, one event in particular stands out, and will always remain, in my memory—chiefly because it so delighted Jimmie.

In one small town, where Jimmie was holding his usual extemporaneous reception before the show, I left his side saying: "I'll go back to the dressing room and lay out your things, Jimmie."

As usual, Jimmie responded: "All right, Mother."

And immediately a stranger, his eyes wide in astonishment, asked: "Pardon me for asking—but is she really your mother?"

That was one time when Jimmie couldn't get back to the dressing room fast enough.

CHAPTER FORTY-ONE

"They call me the yodeling ranger—

"My badge is solid gold—

"I rove the land—by the old Rio Grande—

"And belong to that old ranger fold—."

My husband, Jimmie Rodgers, was sitting on the top rung of his "silver ladder," in undisputed possession—but he was not finished with his struggle; his pitiful long-drawn-out battle with a pitiless opponent. Stubbornly, gallantly, he fought it. If downed, he would say: " Doggone it—I'm going to get up from here. Bring me my clothes, somebody!"

So he would command—in a voice often pathetically weak and shaking. If up, he would protest: "No, now, Mother—I'm all right. Don't you worry, Sugar. Just— just let me rest—a few minutes. Kinda tired. No, now—I'm not goin' to bed. Just want to lie down a minute. Tell 'em I'll be there for my act. Folks have come long ways—some of 'em—. Ain't goin' to disappoint 'em—." His words would trail away in a moaning whisper.

Jimmie was certainly a most impatient patient! But then, he hotly resented being called a patient. Strangely, he'd tell the whole world, gailey, about his troubles with that old T B; but it pleased him to hope that folks really thought he was strong and well. He couldn't forget that once he'd been a bronze-faced, sturdy-bodied young fellow, twisting the wheel, pulling pins, riding the decks in the wind, fog, sleet or sun—and caroling lustily above the squeal of the rails, the clattering chatter of empties.

MY HUSBAND, JIMMIE RODGERS

Then would come a few days, perhaps even a few weeks, when it would seem he was saying to himself: "Hot doggy. Got him down now. Hey-hey!"

But whether weak or strong, he adhered to the tradition of the theater; the show must go on.

"The show," for him, would be more recordings, continuous broadcasting here and there, all over the country; or presenting his act on stages, large or small, in cities or in crossroads villages. Made him no never mind! And—those appealing fan letters; they cheered him, spurred him on. The fans; they'd made everything possible, all this success. If by answering their appeals he could, in turn, make them happy—relieve their loneliness—give them renewed courage.

Many happenings, eventful to us, had occurred during the years '29 to '32. We had gone to Hollywood, and there Jimmie, with Ralph Peer, had been entertained at lunch by Hal Roach, and had met the lovable screen comedians, Laurel and Hardy.

He had made a talking short for Columbia. *The Singing Brakeman*—the best selling short of its time. And when I saw it for the first time, it gave me the same thrill I'd had in that magic second-story of the "brick" in Bristol when I'd first listened to my darling's voice—on the playback. And Mitchie, going to college in the Capital City, had seen it quite by accident. She had gone to see a feature picture, without noticing what else was billed. Didn't even know he had made a talkie. According to her, she nearly fainted with excitement; and not a soul with her to share it.

I've always wished I might have a copy of this film, the only one he ever made, because his strength was unequal to the strain of making others. I'd like to have his voice—just conversational talking; as well as his voice in melody. I remember it was a depot lunch room setting. And on the callboard he'd had them chalk up— the actual names of some of his former railroad buddies: Martin, Harper, Strobel; Oliver—Engine 6977—10:15 A.M.

He sang, too, of course: "Waiting for a Train," "Dear Old Dad" and—"T for

Texas." Still shooting poor Thelma—just to see her jump and fall.

Two of the Victor records have him saying just a few words, in his natural speaking voice. One of them: "The Carter Family Visits Jimmie Rodgers," a recording which has not been released, and of which I have only a sample record, I like especially—because of that little laugh of his; a sort of clipped chuckle. It's there; then it's gone—but I play that record over and over—just to hear my boy—just to hear—that little laugh—.

Too, he had "helped" Will Horwitz, Houston's well-loved philanthropist-showman, open the famous Border station at Reynosa, Mexico—XED. There we had seen—and not liked—our only bullfight.

He had been made a captain in the Ranger Force, State of Texas—honorary. He proudly wore his gold badge, a five-pointed star, with one letter of the word "Texas" for each point. He had been "called" as a Ranger, by Adjutant General William Sterling, to a great Rotarian gathering in Austin, and had presented his superior officer with a Jimmie Rodgers Special Weymann guitar. In all this he had taken the delight of a small boy.

We had been entertained by Major Gordon W. Lillie—"Pawnee Bill"—at his home in Pawnee, Oklahoma, where the famous showman has established his quaint Old Town and Indian Trading Post. Pawnee Bill had insisted on Jimmie eating at least one bite of buffalo meat. The buffalo had been killed a few months before—but that wasn't the reason why Jimmie hesitated and eyed it askance. He knew the meat had been "cured," but he just naturally didn't enjoy experimenting with strange foods. Good old Southern eats for him!

But—he had to be courteous. Pawnee Bill chuckled then—and presented him with a beautiful rug, made from the hide of that very same buffalo, the head mounted "as natural as life, Ma. See it? Say, that's fine!"

Later Major Lillie also sent him a gun and gun-box which he, himself, prized highly as a keepsake—but which he wanted Jimmie to have. The box had been made to hold the three guns which Pawnee Bill had used in his act, for twenty years or more, shooting from horseback; and the gun, of course, was one of the three. Also, he gave Jimmie a china mug which had belonged to Buffalo Bill, Col. William F. Cody. It is really a stein, covered with Masonic emblems in colors, and dated Rochester, N.Y., 1911. And from the time Jimmie became the proud owner of that treasure, he refused to eat his cornbread and milk unless it was served in that stein.

Jimmie had also been made a noble of the Mystic Shrine, Alzafar Temple, May 5, 1931. In presenting a Shrine pin his friend, Werner Tauch, had fastened it to a card; a card bearing a fine friendship verse and the picture of a ship in full sail, all exquisitely hand-illuminated in delicate colors. Framed, this card was one of my Jimmie's treasures. Everybody still admires it.

When the new "Majestic," in San Antonio had its gala opening week with an all-headline bill, Jimmie Rodgers, humble yodeler, topped the list. An ace vaudeville circuit had switched its bookings to enable him to do so.

And his good friend, the late Mayor Chambers, with other officials of the quaint old, yet always new, City of San Antonio de Bexar, made Jimmie Rodgers an honorary member of the "special police," which permitted him, to his huge delight, to install a police siren on his Cadillac.

And a traffic cop, unknowing that the famous Jimmie Rodgers was a "private detective," got the surprise of his life one time when an arrogant motorist ran a red light just as Jimmie and I reached the busy intersection. Seeing the harassed cop doing his best to handle traffic, and blowing his whistle frantically after the fleeing lawbreaker, Jimmie called: "Want me to catch him?"

At the cop's instant nod, Jimmie opened up that siren—and the amazed cop opened his mouth. But—traffic halted; our Cadillac sped after the culprit, and within a few blocks ran him down. But no wonder the cop, and everybody else, was astonished. They were not accustomed to seeing a big, privately-owned sedan suddenly open up a police siren!

In those days—about every six months, I think, Jimmie bought himself a new car! Just like a child tiring of his toys after the newness is gone, he would see another that he longed to own. But—he had so little real enjoyment; could so seldom enjoy what he did have. His "time was not long." We didn't speak of that—but we both knew. And I am so glad he was able to have them.

He bought a Cadillac V-12 Phaeton; a special in Samarkand gray, with trim of Mandalay blue; his blue. This "set him back" considerable, but if somebody had presented him with an all-aluminum stream-lined train, I doubt if he could have enjoyed its possession more. He bought a beautiful Chrysler Eight Imperial sedan, and was immensely proud.

Then, in May of 1932, he bought a beautiful black Cadillac sedan—but this was for me. My Packard was still good, but he thought it was sort of out-dated by then.

But of all Jimmie's cars during this period from '29 to '32, it was "Thirsty, the Christmas Tree," which was his real pal. A shining Ford touring wearing every gleaming gadget Jimmie could possibly figure out a place for. He so thoroughly enjoyed the company of men. He loved stag trips. And Thirsty was always ready and anxious to "take a little trip to the Border." Jimmie's friend, Earle Moore, was his booking agent at that time. With Thirsty they made a joyous trio.

And then—on a Tuesday afternoon, back in January of 1931, a "regular feller," wearing a blue serge suit, a felt hat, an unruly forelock and an infectious grin, took a look at Blue Yodeler's Paradise and queried: "Well, Jimmie—make all this with your throat?"

CHAPTER FORTY-TWO

"I'll feast on the meats—

"And the honey so sweet—

"Away out—on the mountain—."

The night before, a cowhand and a brakie had stood grinning at each other—while a huge mass of human beings had ovationed them both. And the cowhand told several thousand folks, confidentially; "He's my distant son."

A guy from Oklahoma-California and a guy from Mississippi-Texas. A fellow from Oolagah-Hollywood and a fellow from Meridian-Kerrville. The voices of both—infectious humor; heart-throb yodels—known and loved from Sheboygan to Singapore, Long Beach to London, Holyoke to Honolulu, Battle Creek to Buenos Aires. Will Rogers. Jimmie Rodgers.

Two men; each clinging stubbornly to the belief: "The underest dog is just as good as I am; and I'm just as good as the toppest dog."

Winging over the hills and plains of Texas on an errand of mercy, Will Rogers had come down out of the sky that drizzly 26th of January, 1931.

To do his bit, to give what service he might, Jimmie Rodgers had come down from his shanty—away out on the mountain.

There was no feasting on meats and honey so sweet in the lost corners of the beautiful State of Arkansas that bleak winter following those long months of searing drouth, the summer of 1930. Human beings sat helpless and hopeless in tiny log cabins in drouth-burnt clearings, their last poke of meal gone.

194

MY HUSBAND, JIMMIE RODGERS

So now, the famous Red Cross tour for the benefit of those desolate human beings, a tour conceived and headed by the World's Ambassador of Wit, and sponsored by the noted financier-publishers, Jesse H. Jones, of Houston, and Amon G. Carter, of Fort Worth, and the well-known Texan, Houston Harte, of San Angelo, was underway. In rain and mud, ironically enough!

For some time Jimmie and I had read, with growing distress, various newspaper accounts of the pathetic plight of those humble cabin homes. He had railroaded some through the state. We had driven through it many times. And he had showed the larger cities; Little Rock and Hot Springs.

At last Jimmie told me: "Carrie—we'll drive up there; make a swing through the larger towns. I'll give the entire proceeds of my performances—and pay my own expenses—give all I make to whatever organization is trying to relieve those poor devils."

So we were planning; and then over the radio we learned of the Will Rogers tour. And Jimmie Rodgers commented with a pleased grin: "Gosh—that's great!" And he added wistfully: "Gee, I wish I could help."

I asked him: "Why not?"

Jimmie just looked at me—sort of shocked. He said: "Gee—not with Will Rogers!" As if he were saying: "Not with—the King of England!"

But I persisted: "No, Jimmie—you know he's a—well, what you call a regular guy. If he can find a place for you on his program, he'll appreciate your offer, maybe—if you make it."

Jimmie was very doubtful. Still, he said: "Maybe he might let me help—let me appear with him in Santone the 26th, anyway. I'd feel as if I was doing something— even if just one performance. He's goin' to carry some other entertainers with him: Chester Byers, the famous trick roper—and The Revellers. Gosh—that'll be some show! But I don't reckon he'd want me—."

"I'd wire him, anyway, if I were you. Can't do any harm."

So Jimmie Rodgers timidly sent a wire to the great humorist, saying among other things: "If you have room for me on your program, I gladly offer my services, not only here but any place."

And Will Rogers wired back to the young master of Blue Yodeler's Paradise: "Many thanks to you—."

Few can realize, perhaps, just what all this meant to us. Just four years ago we had faced each other in that city, a broke brakie with T B, and a young wife and little tot—and three dimes.

Now—the Gunter. The Crystal Ballroom. Crowds—jams. Officials, society, clubs. The great and near-great of the city; of all South Texas. Officers in uniform from the fort and the flying fields. Members of the Old Trail Drivers Association. Just everybody who counted—and Jimmie, humbly grateful to be just a part of it. And I was elated to be just an onlooker, remaining in the background as much as I could—just for the joy of watching everybody and everything.

Until "the gang" all trekked to the beautiful Municipal Auditorium I had scarcely a glimpse of Jimmie; but wherever he might be, I knew he was, for the moment, enjoying himself to the fullest—and I was so proud of him.

It was Will Rogers' college-boy son, Will, Junior, who escorted us around; a likeable youngster who won my heart instantly when he confided to me how crazy he was about all my Jimmie's records. I knew a little secret thrill when Will, Junior, stepped to the box office and explained briefly just "who we were." You see, my husband and Will Rogers had both been too busy, too rushed, to remember "who we were."

And—Will Rogers explained to the folks "out front" that Jimmie Rodgers was his distant son; and a good time "was had by all."

Next morning, Tuesday, out to Winburn Field to board the trimotored Ford, loaned temporarily by The Aviation Corporation until the noted flier, Frank Hawks, loaned by The Texas Company, could join the party with "The Hell Diver."

A benefit tour for drouth sufferers—and the plane bogged down in mud!

What to do! San Angelo—"something like three hundred miles, ain't it? Gotta make it. Frank'll meet us there, maybe. Gotta make it, sure."

They made it in my Packard and another car. While I, unknowing, shopped leisurely with Nita and my friend, Mrs. Powell, and discovered, when it came time to go home, that we had no transportation.

Home, then, to Kerrville—to find a mighty busy "cullud gal" in the kitchen putting away stacks of china; a proud, beaming Anna, telling me all about the impromptu stag luncheon. Will Rogers—the one and only! And Jimmie Rodgers playing host. I sat—just wanting to cry from happiness—knowing how he had felt about that.

And the following November, the world-famous humorist phoned my Jimmie, asking him to meet him at the Gunter to help him celebrate his birthday. I don't know what they ate—chili, I suppose—but Will Rogers sent me his splendid birthday cake.

Jimmie was unable to make the entire scheduled tour, owing to contracts, recording and others, to be filled, but it was a grand time for him.

Often and often, when he was sick, he asked for the picture they'd posed together, Will Rogers and he, in front of our home. He was proud of it. I am too, of course, but it saddens me more than any other picture of him. He appears so jaunty in his fine "Texas" hat and light gray flannels. His smile is pleased, yet wistful. One has but to study this picture—to note the frailty of the body under that natty suit—merely glance at the thin, wasting hands—to see that even then, he was dying.

And a news photo, made some time while he was still on that errand of mercy, shows plainly the strain of the effort he was making to do "any little thing he could to help the suffering." He had done his bit—at great sacrifice.

When my good brown Anna had run all out of chuckling little comments, that January evening, about "dem boys—jes crazy—jes like lit' bitsy boys"—and "dat Mistah Will; don't nothin' make him no nevah mind; he jes lak—lak jes anybody," I was restless, lonesome.

But—maybe they'd be on the air. No-o—, but KMAC had on a Jimmie Rodgers record:

"There's a little red house—on top of a hill—not very far—from an old syrup mill—."

CHAPTER FORTY-THREE

"I'm goin' to town—

"What you want me to bring you

"Bring a pint of booze—

"And a John B. Stetson hat—."

"Throw your things together, kid. We're leaving here for there."

Not the same words. The old gay command not quite so gay. But the meaning was the same.

Jimmie had once said: "After prowlin' all over creation, I've decided Kerrville's about the prettiest place I ever struck. Shucks—I can just lazy 'round, fish and swim, an' climb the hills. Got lots of pretty drives around here, too—and Kerrville folks sure are fine. Mighty good to us."

But Jimmie simply couldn't "just lazy 'round." And a frail young man can do little swimming in swift streams; little hill climbing, no matter how sweet the air, how lovely the ferns, how joyous the birds.

"Mother, I've got a plot of ground in Santone. Mighty pretty location. High. You'll like it. In Alamo Heights."

A sick boy's need for new interests. Something new to think about, plan for. A plot of ground. Another shanty to be excited about. We'd live there a year or so, maybe. Then—if he lived—where? New Orleans? Miami? Los Angeles? If he—lived—.

"You see, Mother, I like Kerrville fine; but—it's just a bit too inconvenient for us. You think I'm right, don't you, Mother? I want you to be happy. If you'd rather stay here—."

I could see he was right. "Go to town." That's what both of us were doing eternally. Shows, shopping, visiting, pleasure, business. And—that extra drive to The Heart o' the Hills was just too much for him sometimes; although he wouldn't mention that.

"Yes, Jimmie. I know you're right. But—let's not have a big house this time. How about a duplex? With nice people in the other half? Then we can be free to go places, stay as long as we please. Just turn the key—and forget it."

So—goodbye to Blue Yodeler's Paradise. What if I did cry—in secret? My tears, my regrets, my small-girl distress over my pretty toy being mine no longer—were my secret. But that big fine home was just that—a pretty toy. Better, much better, that my boy could be where the things he needed—when he had to yield to weakness and take to his bed—were instantly obtainable. A specialist, a nurse, could be there within twenty minutes at most.

"Now this is fine, Mother. Just my kind of a home. Don't have to walk blocks—through my own house—to see what it looks like. Handy for our friends to drop in overnight, or for an hour, anyway—when they drive through, goin' to the Coast. Up there—well, they just about had to take a day off; or just go on. And I sure enjoy havin' 'em come see me."

They came. And many of his fans came—when they learned his address. Also letters came, and little gifts—from his fans. Little homey gifts—from his kind of folks. And radio stars like Johnny Marvin broke broadcasting rules—to send him through the ether cheery messages; and to dedicate their songs to him—"to our Jimmie, who's sick down in San Antonio, Texas—."

And a fan wrote many pages, urging: "Get well, Jimmie. We just don't see how we can go on without our Jimmie's voice to listen to—."

Then slow tears would well up in the sick boy's brown eyes, and he would pray aloud to his Master to let him live—just a while longer—"But—if you say you want me—."

Messages, telegrams, long distance and local calls. When do you think he'll be on

MY HUSBAND, JIMMIE RODGERS

the air again? Yes—his records played in the studios are fine—but we like to know he's there himself. We enjoy his little comments. Will he be able to make that appearance here? Here—there—everywhere.

Presently: "My new suit come yet? No, now, I'm all right, Mother. I'm goin' to get up from here. Goin' to the barber shop—an' I want to make the rounds—. And tomorrow I gotta drive over to—Say, Sugar, phone the studio, will you, and tell 'em I'll be there for my broadcast tonight."

And there would be Mickey; a delighted wriggling Mickey. "Hi, fella. How's the boy?" Man and his dog. A boy and his playfellow.

And there would be Nita. "Gosh. Gettin' most as tall as her Ma. How's your report cards? Tell Daddy the truth, now."

Then the two of us, my husband holding me close to him, arms so weak, but so strong with devotion. His thin cheek against my head for a moment. His voice earnest: "Gee, Carrie. You don't know how happy I am. My two!"

And in October we drove to Mississippi; to attend a golden wedding anniversary. And Jimmie said, his voice, his words, most solemn:

"Some way I've got a feeling that the next time we're in Meridian—it will be for—a different reason."

Was he thinking of his beloved Dad? Or had he some premonition that he might—.

Never before had he hinted that any sorrow might be in store for us—for me.

CHAPTER FORTY-FOUR

"And I can't forget the time—

"When I asked you to be mine—."

October the twenty-ninth. A golden wedding day. My Dad's and Mother's. Reverend J. T. Williamson. Kizzie Ann Davidson.

Never no mo' blues, this day! Golden smiles, golden laughter. And nothing blue—except the Delta skies; and blue eyes, and Jimmie's now famous blue bow tie.

Gold. Gold icing for the cake. Candles of gold. Ribbons of gold. Great feathery golden mums. Little gifts of gold. Even—heads of gold; our lively Nita's silky gold bob, and Mitchie's auburn hair and tiny golden freckles.

Fifty golden years Dad and Mother had traveled the road together. Here, now gathered around them, every one of their nine children, the husbands or wives of eight of them, and most of the grandchildren. The Master had beckoned some of them, including our little June Rebecca—but of Dad's and Mother's own flesh and blood, not one was missing that day.

Their youngest, our schoolgirl Mitchie, was the only one who had not—as yet—presented them with a son-in-law or daughter-in-law. But Dad said, gravely, his eyes crinkling: "Give her time."

So—no sad thoughts for this day. Teasing jibes. Proud smiles. A few tender tears—of happiness. Grateful thanks to their Heavenly Father who had guided them, provided for them, rewarded them.

MY HUSBAND, JIMMIE RODGERS

Groups clustered around the piano, singing. Jimmie Rodgers, with his famous old guitar, strumming, plinking, crooning. Grandchildren scampering, screaming at play. Mickey excited; under somebody's feet every minute; being grabbed up in admiring arms—wriggling, kissing.

A grand day for everybody. And an especially grand day for America's Blue Yodeler. A home. Family. More than all else, those were the things that meant real happiness to Jimmie Rodgers. Kids. Dogs. Old friends. Neighbors. Folks. His kind of folks.

Though tired, he was supremely content. When night came on, a soft southern night, he was content—just to sit huddled on the front steps, enjoying his smoke, just "talkin' 'bout this and that" with the menfolk of his family.

Somebody brought him a banjo. His long fingers plinked and plunked, drawing magic as sweet as that which he drew from his old guitar for the delight of millions.

Then, for his homefolks, he crooned: "O, the Mississippi moon—is shining down tonight—an' love just seems—to fill the air—."

Hearing that, Elsie McWilliams, the family poetess, appeared in the lighted doorway; Elsie who had composed the words of that tender little ballad.

Seeing her, Jimmie sent her a very special smile; and added impishly: "Yodel-ay-ee-ee—."

CHAPTER FORTY-FIVE

"I still love—

"And you know I do—

"Sweetheart—I always will—."

"My time ain't long."

He could sing that, moaning cheerfully, but he would not say it.

I am convinced that he knew it, that winter of '32-'33. Perhaps his Master had whispered to him: "Better be in readiness, Jimmie Boy. I'll be calling you home— pretty soon, now—."

His gravity, those days, even when not in pain, was most unusual. He seemed anxious to explain to me at considerable length all the details of business. What to do in case—not using those words, however—. Anxious to be assured that when he laid down his guitar—forever—his two would not be faced with a maze of difficulties; of tangled business affairs. And I gave him my promise—to do the best I could about writing his story—"if anything happens so I don't get it done, Mother."

With his adored little daughter, Anita, he had been always, whenever strong enough to be on his feet, such a teasing, laughing playmate. Laughing with her; romping with her; teaching her to drive; even roller skating with her sometimes.

But—never had I known him to be the "heavy father"; to pin her down to listen to solemn parental advice. That was not his way. But now—on a day in January, I chanced to overhear my husband in a bit of drawn-aside conversation with his girl-child; kindly, fatherly advice about her little schoolboy friends; about not bothering

Mother too much with things that don't matter.

And at last I heard him say—just two simple words; two words to sum up all that he wished, hoped her to be. And I doubt if any venerable scholar with all the words of all the tongues of the ages at his command, could give to his daughter any better advice than Jimmie Rodgers, humble railroad man, unassuming yodeler, gave to his girl child that day.

Just these two simple words: "Keep sweet."

As for me, I'd begun to lose my terror—about that old T B. It had sort of begun to seem now that because of his indomitable spirit, because of his intense will-to-live, my husband would outlive me—many years. Not that I phrased it that way, even to myself. But—I'd gotten over asking myself, when we told each other a gay, tender goodbye: "Will he come back alive—or—?"

He'd be bedfast for weeks. Then—he'd be up. More trouping. Another recording. And as soon as I could, I'd join him, on such rare occasions as I hadn't accompanied him all the way.

In the spring of 1933 came a month in the hospital. Then three months at home, in bed. And then:

"Goin' to New York, Mother. Old contract's up. Gotta talk it over with Ralph. See what he thinks about that Brunswick offer. Won't take it, though, if Victor meets it. Victor—they've been fine to me. Only thing is—gotta have more money. Doctors, nurses, hospitals—doggone! They cost a lot, don't they?

"Got to record twelve more numbers, too. Sorry I had to keep 'em waitin' so long.

"If I go by boat, Ma, I can come back by train; stop over and visit Annie and Alex on the way. Nita's school will be out by then, and I can bring her on home from Meridian with me. Wish it was so you could go too, Carrie."

But—there were two reasons why I couldn't, just then. One was my brother, Covert. We had urged him to come to Texas. He, too, needed dry healing air for sick lungs; needed a higher altitude, warm sunshine. Too long he had delayed obeying medical advice; a change of climate. Perhaps we could save him.

The other—and very important—reason was frankly a question of expenses. It was necessary now for Jimmie to have a trained nurse in constant attendance; her fare and expenses, besides her salary, must be paid—wherever he went. Aside from being within call, on that trip, there would be nothing I could do.

He would be gone only a week or so; three at the most. Then he and Nita would be home. And—perhaps poor brother Covert would get well—.

So—at the Sunset Station, here in the Alamo City, my young husband held me close in his arms, in the semi-darkness of a Pullman platform, and told me: "Girl, you don't know what you've meant to me; what you'll always mean to me—as long as I live. Everything that's fine and true and sweet."

Two people in each other's arms. The hiss of steam—a uniformed nurse, a uniformed porter approaching. Then I was alone—and a Southern Pacific train was speeding through the night—toward Galveston, where would be the *S.S. Mohawk*.

Alone? No—there was Covert. Must have a specialist. And there was my boy's beloved Mickey—Mickey McDonald Rodgers, a gift to Jimmie from his good friends, Mr. and Mrs. Charles McDonald, of Mt. Pleasant.

Mickey; registered Boston bull, a handsome little fellow, who had his own radio fans. It delighted Jimmie to let Mickey "talk" into the mike at broadcasting stations. And it pleased him immensely when Mickey got fan letters. Jimmie loved Mickey more than any of all the fine dogs he'd ever owned.

Before the train left I'd begged the nurse: "Please don't let Jimmie expend an ounce of energy trying to write me even so much as a postcard. Make him rest and relax every minute you possibly can. But—you send me word, every single day, telling me just how he's getting along. Don't even ask him what to say. Just tell me.

MY HUSBAND, JIMMIE RODGERS

So I won't worry."

But—just try to keep my husband from writing me, no matter how sick or weak he might be! The ship had scarcely left Galveston before he was penning a letter to me: "Somehow I am lonesome. Guess I'll feel better tomorrow—sure hope Covert is feeling good—it seems I miss my sweethearts more and more every day—."

Every day some message, never forgetting a thoughtful word for Covert. "I feel bad about Covert. I believe if I were there I could help him lots. Tell him to make himself comfortable the way he sees best until I get home. And if I were him I would smoke my cigarettes or anything else I wanted to—smoke because it helps make him contented. If he will spray his throat heavy and deep with some good antiseptic after every smoke it will help him lots. Happiness and contentment are the best things on earth for his and my kind—and I haven't got any better sense than to be both.—Write me Washington next."

So—I wrote him—to Washington: Wrote and told him all the little everyday happenings about home and friends, the things he so loved to have me write when he was away. But—that letter—.

He had made his twelve recordings; all perfect; all masters. His voice under perfect control; never a break.

One of the most persistent questions about Jimmie Rodgers was how, with that T B cough, could he sing so well? How could his voice remain so clear and sweet; so round and full? Well—following medical advice, and because he'd found it was the one thing that would permit him to use his voice for a few moments at a time without the annoyance and embarrassment of that distressing cough, he would take a big swallow of good bonded whiskey immediately before singing.

So—after five years as their best selling star, Victor had given Jimmie a new contract—at a better figure than ever. And he had made for them twelve fine recordings; one to be released each month for a year.

MY HUSBAND, JIMMIE RODGERS

He could come home now and rest. At last he saw the need of just resting for a while in some good sanitarium.

At last, for a little time, perhaps, he would be content to sit in the sun—with folded hands.

He would return by train so he could stop over in Meridian and bring our daughter home—our Nita. We'd had to let her go to Grandma's that spring, to finish her school year there. I'd been on the road with Jimmie. Sister Gladys had taken charge of our home—and our daughter—for a time, that winter, but she'd been called back to Meridian. It had seemed best to let her take Nita.

Soon, now, within a very few days, both my darlings would be home. And Covert and I were planning. He was feeling a little better, but needed almost constant care and attention—just as Jimmie had.

A little package came. A box of candy. On the flap cover Jimmie had penned: "(Over)." On the under side: "I love you, Sweetheart. Your daddy." That was all. Just a little-boy surprise message. Just a bit of tender thoughtfulness from a devoted husband. And I remembered that his very first present to me had been a box of candy, personally delivered by a husky young railroad man.

May. It had been May when Jimmie Rodgers had made his first broadcast in Asheville.

A year later, in May, I bought an immense scrap book in Washington. Now, in May, in San Antonio, at last I'd found what I'd been searching for; an exact duplicate of that first book.

Raining—that twenty-fifth of May. Covert seemed to be resting comfortably, but so weak.

A letter—from Nita, telling me how she'd just been down to the Union Station there in Meridian to post a letter to her Daddy, so maybe he'd get it before he left for Washington, on his way home. Grandma'd gone with her, she said. And she'd told Grandma: "Just think! Next time I come to this station I'll be coming to meet my Daddy."

Raining. I could spend the day getting my darling's press notices all in orderly array. Those bundles and boxes of clippings, piling up through the years, waiting for the second big book, ever since that first had been filled—in less than a year.

I wanted to write to my boy, and I wanted to write to Nita. So many things to tell them; seemed I couldn't wait. But—no use. They'd be home before my letters could reach them.

And I told my boy's pal, that wriggly Mickey: "He'll be here soon now, Boy. Our Daddy and Nita—soon be home."

As I sorted and arranged the clippings it came to me how oddly that month of May kept recurring. So many things of interest to us, personally at least, had happened in May. That first broadcast. Buying his first pressbook. Not finding a second to match until now—five years later in May. Buying our first Cadillac sedan—in May. Jimmie made a noble of the Mystic Shrine—in May. And now, he had finished making another recording—in May. And he'd be coming back home—in May.

And then I remembered that one of the very most important events of our thirteen years together had happened in April. Just a few weeks before Jimmie had gone to New York this last time we'd celebrated our thirteenth wedding anniversary. Being just a little superstitious, I couldn't help saying to myself, with a little sigh: "I'll be thankful when we've gotten safely past our fourteenth year."

Press notices; clippings from newspapers, from magazines of national circulation. Many of them several columns each. Interviewers, columnists, reviewers. Likening the story of Jimmie Rodgers to a Horatio Alger tale. "In spite of unpromising, uncolorful beginnings, now—before he is thirty—plays upon the heartstrings of millions the world over with as little effort as he once brought response from the first stringed musical instrument his sensitive fingers ever caressed; a cheap, second-hand ukelele."

"Incredible; within a few months' time, a miraculous but steady stream of gold being poured into the still boyish hands of this happy-hearted ex-brakie who yodels sobbingly of past trials and tribulations."

"Truth in that heart-throb voice. Truth behind those doleful songs. In times of heartbreak or of suffering, Jimmie Rodgers sings."

Reading these, again I recalled that time when, during a pathetic period of intense suffering, he had picked up his old guitar and strumming with pitifully white fingers, his voice weak but goldenly clear, he had sung: "We'll sing—sing—sing—the doles away—." And he had told me, grinning weakly: "Daggone, Mother. That'll be a dandy—when I get it worked out good."

Other reviewers said: "Yodeler extraordinary. Novel entertainment of the South, by the South, and for true Southerners. Negro spirituals sung in syncopated rhythm—better known as blues—."

"Passages referring to homesickness, loneliness and blues arose from his own unhappy experiences when he was unknown, ill, jobless, a tramp hunting work—."

Recalling those times now saddened me. My darling was no longer a tramp; no longer a homeless unknown. He was America's Blue Yodeler. But he was still battling—defying that old T B. I pasted that clipping in its proper place. Then my hands held something that was not a clipping; a scrap or stationery with a penciled scrawl.

I smoothed it out—and suddenly remembered Jimmie Rodgers in his sunny room at Blue Yodeler's Paradise; with a little new Bible beside him. He was making a rough draft of what he wanted to pen on the flyleaf of the little new book. Some way that rough draft had become mixed with his press clippings. I smiled a little, now, remembering how he'd worried over those few words. He was so earnestly anxious to have it just right—this little inscription for his daughter's Bible.

MY HUSBAND, JIMMIE RODGERS

"To my sweet little daughter, Miss Carrie Anita Rodgers, who was born January 30th, 1921. I hope you live by and obey this book always. From your Daddy who loves you dearly—Jimmie Rodgers."

Back then to my pasting, but my eyes lingered now and then over the lines.

"Fine lovable grown-up boy who loves his dog. If announced President coming—couldn't stir up more excitement. Tunes that linger with you long after you've heard them. Sophisticated in the manner of a railroad man. No affectation; no smack of Broadway or Hollywood. Everything about him is a heart-throb. Wistfully old-fashioned just like his songs. Reminiscent of the eighties; of wistaria clad cottages. Whistle of an engine—his inspiration. When asked about Mrs. Jimmie, his face radiated a glow: 'The sweetest and dearest little lady in the world and the most precious little daughter anywhere are waiting for me.'"

I'm not ashamed to say, when I came to that one, before pasting it in the book, I held it to my lips a moment; and I told my darling, across a thousand miles or more of America: "We are, Honey. We are—waiting for you to come home."

It didn't matter that our Nita was in Meridian and I here in San Antonio. We were both waiting for him; both had so many exciting things to tell him; both longing to know again that wistful smile, that teasing gaiety—even when he wasn't feeling extra good—.

Mickey wriggled delightedly, as usual, when he heard Jimmie's voice—but it was only a record I'd put on the Orthophonic: "The Home Call."

Listening to my Jimmie's voice, I sat up half the night pasting and pasting; determined to complete my task. He'd be so pleased!

So late when I finally tumbled into bed. So very long before I could go to sleep—my thoughts completely with my darling—happy thoughts—.

Six o'clock in the morning!

The telephone—ringing—ringing—ringing—!

MY HUSBAND, JIMMIE RODGERS

Long distance—New York calling.

Calling Mrs. Jimmie Rodgers!

Hotel Taft—

Tubercular pneumonia—

May! The twenty-sixth day of May, in the Year of Our Lord, Nineteen Hundred and Thirty-Three—.

"Lay aside your old guitar, now, Jimmie—Come home—to Me—and rest—."

"I keep all his letters—

"I keep his gold ring, too—."

EPILOGUE

"Meridian next time—for a different reason—."

"—This station next time, Grandma—to meet my Daddy!"

They were both right, my two.

Union Station. Folks. Lots of folks. Soft southern night. Everything a blur. Numb. I could see nothing; hear nothing. Yet I seemed to see everything; hear everything through a dark blueness.

Then—like a part of the night itself, a low, mellow train whistle. Not the usual "whoo-whoo-oo," but a whistle that was not a whistle. A long, continuous moaning that grew in volume as the train crept toward me along the silver rails.

"Whoo-oo-oo-oo-oo—."

Continuous; never ceasing until the powerful engine breathed to a rest and the drivers ceased turning.

Tribute! The train crew; engineer, fireman, all of them—remembered how Jimmie Rodgers had loved train whistles.

Through the open doors of a coach I saw flowers; waxy white, and an enormous bow of ribbon. Blue; Jimmie's blue, a dreamy, smoky blue, like his blue yodels.—A card: R. S. Peer.

Somebody was saying: "Scottish Rite Cathedral, until Monday afternoon—then—First Methodist Episcopal Church—and Oak Grove—the sunset hour—."

May, the twenty-ninth. The sunset hour. "Underneath the Mississippi Moon." My Jimmie—resting beside his little dark-eyed baby.

Home-ward—to the home of my father and mother. Somewhere along the way a bungalow—a Victrola—a song—"O, the Mississippi moon is smiling down to-night—." And I learned then what torture meant.

Aware of our passing, some kindly hand lifted the needle—quickly. But, too late. I'd heard. The others with me—my little daughter—all of us had heard. But—we knew that somebody in that little bungalow treasured that record more than ever, now.

And we realized that we'd be hearing it—and other records—often and often. To avoid letting others torture us unknowingly, we knew then that we had to accustom ourselves. The sooner, the better.

Grimly, determinedly, we formed a group around the Victrola, telling each other we'd play them all—as soon as possible. Whether the first record happened to be one of the rowdiest, gaiest—or one of the loneliest and tenderest. No matter.

Somebody warned in a low voice: "Cut it off. She's—." But I said: "No. Play it— to the last note—." Then as Mother moved toward me, anxiously, I said: "No, now, Mother—I'm all right." And shuddered a little—remembering. And I saw my child quivering—looking so like Jimmie—.

Then—I was aware of frantic little paws, scratching on the door screen. Somebody said: "He's been sitting right there on those steps for hours, just peering up and down the street. All right, Mickey—coming."

Jimmie's Boston. He came to each of us—but he didn't see us. He was looking for someone else. He'd heard—his pal's voice.

A few days later I was in the house alone for an hour or so. I wanted to be alone.

Suddenly, I wanted Jimmie's music. Not just because it was his, but because his has always pleased me more than any other. If he had never belonged to me I would have been one of his fans, just the same.

I wanted—really yearned—to hear his voice; not just his music.

And suddenly, it came to me: "Why—it's marvelous to think I can have his voice—through all the lonely years. Others treasure letters, keepsakes, kodak pictures. But—I have all those—and his voice, too."

I selected a record. Not "The Home Call." Not—yet. I chose "The Soldier's

MY HUSBAND, JIMMIE RODGERS

Sweetheart"; his first.

Four hours later I awoke from the first restful sleep—one not induced by seda-tives—I'd known since that long distance call from New York.

Tributes. Poems inspired by his songs, his life. Songs—to him, of him, sung over the radio.

The RCA Victor Company issued Jimmie Rodgers records bearing his portrait and signature. Some new photographic process. I wish he could have seen them; he would have been so pleased. But—they were too fragile. Only a comparatively few were made.

Tributes from columnists. The daily press. Showfolk, in their canvas church, at their annual sunrise memorial service for troupers who have taken their last curtain. Prayers—for my Jimmie and others—.

One tribute might not seem such an honor to some folks; but Jimmie's folks were all kinds. He liked all kinds. So I know he would be pleased if he could know that even in far-away Central America a rum was named for him; just as he was so pleased when proud parents named their precious boy-babies for him: Jimmie Rodgers Smith—or Jimmie Rodgers Wilson. He had such a small-boy pleasure in any little token of appreciation; like the modest country flowers in a shoe box—"for you."

So—he'd like knowing about the rum. Make him no never mind—what others might think or say. Yes—he'd have liked to sample it, too. "Jimmie Rodgers Rum; Companie Vinicola Hispano Americano, Panama City."

And—he'd like to know that his Baybo cherishes that little Bible. "Keep sweet."

My tribute? Jimmie's book. I've done the best I could to keep my promise—in case anything happened so he didn't get it written. I've done what he said; just writ-ten it out my own way; just told it in my own words.

And—I'm trying to hold tight to his gay command:

"Chin-chin, Mother."

INDEX

INDEX

INDEX

INDEX

INDEX

INDEX